ISBN 978-1-4400-3934-8
PIBN 10162555

Essays on the Self and Its Powers

By Edward Carpenter

Author of "Towards Democracy," "Civilisation,"
etc. etc.

London: George Allen, *Ruskin House*
156, Charing Cross Road Mdcccciv

Printed by Ballantyne, Hanson & Co.
At the Ballantyne Press

"*These two things, the spiritual and the material, though we call them by different names, in their Origin are one and the same.*"

—Lao-tzŭ.

"*When a new desire has declared itself in the human heart, when a new plexus is forming among the nerves, then the revolutions of nations are already decided, and histories unwritten are written.*"

—Towards Democracy.

PREFACE

We seem to be arriving at a time when, with the circling of our knowledge of the globe, a great synthesis of all human thought on the ancient and ever-engrossing problem of Creation is quite naturally and inevitably taking shape. The world-old wisdom of the Upanishads, with their profound and impregnable doctrine of the universal Self, the teachings of Buddha or of Lao-tzŭ, the poetic insight of Plato, the inspired sayings of Jesus and Paul, the speculations of Plotinus, or of the Gnostics, and the wonderful contributions of later European thought, from the fourteenth century mystics down through Spinoza, Berkeley, Kant, Hegel, Schopenhauer, Ferrier and others; all these, combining with the immense mass of material furnished by modern physical and biological Science, and Psychology, are preparing a great birth, as it were; and out of this meeting of elements is already arising the dim outline of a philosophy which must surely dominate human thought for a long period.

A *new* philosophy we can hardly expect, or wish for; since indeed the same germinal thoughts of the Vedic authors come all the way down history even to Schopenhauer and Whitman, inspiring philosophy after philosophy and religion after religion. But it is only to-day that our knowledge of the world enables us to recognise this immense *consensus;* and it is only to-day that Science, with its huge conquests in the material plane, is able to provide—for these world-old principles—somewhat of a new form, and so wonderful a garment of illustration and expression as it does.

The philosophy of the Upanishads was nothing if not practical; and the same has been said by every great religion of its own teaching. ("Do the will and ye shall know of the doctrine.") It is not sufficient to study and investigate the art of Creation as an external problem; *we have to learn and to practise the art in ourselves.* So alone will it become vital and really intelligible to us. The object of the present volume is to show something of both these sides, the speculative and the practical.

Chapter II., from which the book takes its name, was originally given as an address. The remainder of the body of the book appears now for the first time—with the exception of Chapters VIII. and IX., on "The Gods." These in an altered form were published as an article in the *Hibbert Journal* for Jan. 1904, and for leave to reprint them I am much indebted to the Editor of that Journal. In the Appendix I have included three articles of a considerably earlier date, as possibly in their way contributing some light to the main questions of the book.

E. C.

CONTENTS

APPENDIX

THE ART OF CREATION

I

PRELIMINARY

RELATED Motion seems to be, as suggested by the words Attraction and Repulsion, Gravitation, Chemical Affinity, and so forth, the ground-fact of inorganic Nature. And it seems also to be the ground and foundation of Life. The protoplasmic jelly moves towards or away from substances in its neighborhood, and this appears to be its fundamental property. The most primitive cellular organisms act in the same way. Some seek light, others flee from it. Paramecium is drawn towards slightly acid substances, and flies from alkalies. Actynophrys is attracted by starch; and so on.[1] There appears to be a kind of 'choice' or elective affinity; and the learned are divided on the subject into two schools—those who, like Binet, see in these movements of protozoa the germinal characteristics of human intelligence, and those who class them as "merely chemical" and automatic reactions.

[1] See Th. Ribot, "Psychology of the Emotions," Contemporary Science Series, p. 4. Also H. S. Jennings, "Psychology of a Protozoan," *American Journal of Psychology*, vol. x.

It is not our business here to draw the line of division. It is sufficient to see that on the very lowest rung of the ladder of life, and at a point where it is difficult to distinguish its laws from those of chemistry, such words as we are forced to use—words like Attraction, Repulsion, Affinity—have a double meaning, covering both material and mental, external and internal, affections. Even the word Motion itself passes easily into E-motion. And modern psychology and physiology have made it abundantly clear that every feeling or emotion in the mind means *motion* of some kind in the tissues or fluids of the body. Some of our highest and most complex emotions take the form of attraction or repulsion, and in our dimmest sensations, almost below the level of consciousness, we still can detect the same.

All Nature is motion. In the most primitive Life there is a *tendency* to motion provoked by a neighboring object. This capacity to be provoked into motion is called irritability, and in a higher degree sensibility. All these words—'tendency,' 'irritability,' 'sensibility'—have a mental as well as physical import, which it is difficult to escape from. If a protozoic cell does not feel 'desire' for food such as we feel, it, exhibits a 'tendency' towards it, which we can hardly refuse to regard as the germ of 'desire.'

Over the question of the *priority* of the mental or the material aspects of cells and other things there has been much discussion—some maintaining that chemical and automatic reactions come first, and that later, out of these, mental phenomena are evolved; while others insist that consciousness in some form is prior, and the material world only its expression. I think it best and simplest to suppose the two simultaneous and coextensive—and I shall (provisionally) assume this position, leaving the question to clear itself up later in the book.[1] I may, however, here quote two passages from Lloyd-Morgan's "Introduction to Comparative Psychology."[2] Speaking of consciousness in some form as accompanying all vital organisation, he says: "Does it not seem reasonable to suppose that no matter what stage we select, analysis would still disclose the two aspects? That with the simpler modes of nerve-energy there would go simpler modes of consciousness, and that with infra-neural modes of energy there would be infra-consciousness, or that from which Consciousness as we know it has arisen in process of Evolution?" And again, speaking of a dog as having grown from a single fertilised egg-cell: "From what then have its states of consciousness been evolved? Do we not seem forced by parity of reasoning to answer: From something more simple than consciousness, but of the same order of existence, which answers subjectively to the simpler organic energy of the fertilised ovum"—that is, he supposes that associated with the egg-cell is a subconsciousness of some kind, which expands into the fuller

[1] See chapters iii. and iv.
[2] Contemporary Science Series, pp. 8 and 328.

consciousness *pari passu* with the evolution of the egg-cell into the dog.

Let us assume for the present that Mind and Matter are simultaneous and coextensive. Then on the latter side we have in ascending scale, first, purely inorganic substances (if there are such), then crystals, protoplasmic cells, vegetation, the animal world, man, and whatever beings are superior to man; while on the mental side corresponding we have simple attraction and repulsion, selective affinity, irritability, sensibility, simple consciousness, self-consciousness, and such higher stages of consciousness as are beyond. Taking this view, we are enabled to abandon the somewhat futile attempts which have been made in all ages to *separate* Mind and Matter, and to glorify one over the other (sometimes mind over matter, and sometimes matter over mind). These attempts have led mankind into all sorts of bogs, which we may hope now simply to pass by and leave behind. There is a *distinction* between Mind and Matter (as of two aspects of the same thing), but no real separation.

This subject is dealt with at more length in the chapter on Matter and Consciousness (chap. iii.). We may say here, however, that the distinction between Mind and Matter forces us to conceive, or try to conceive, of a 'stuff' prior to both—a something of which they are the two aspects; and thus we come to the world-old idea of primitive Being (before all differentiation, emanation, or expression), or the 'Will' of the later philosophers (Schopenhauer, Hartmann, Royce, and others). This Will or Being is absolutely not thinkable by the ordinary consciousness (except as a necessary ground for other thoughts), for obviously it lies beyond the region of thought. I shall, however, endeavour to show that it *is* known in the stage of (cosmic) consciousness transcending our ordinary consciousness The perception of matter and mind as distinct things belongs only to our ordinary (self) consciousness. This distinction is not known in the earlier stage of simple consciousness, and it passes away again in the higher and more perfect stage of the cosmic consciousness. (See chap. iv. on "The Three Stages of Consciousness.")

Nevertheless, though Matter and Mind are not separable, and may be regarded as two aspects of one reality, there *are* advantages in cases in treating one as prior to the other. As a rule, since our mental states are the things that are nearest to us and that we know best, it seems wisest to begin from the mental side. Then if we explain material things in terms of mind, we explain things little known in terms of things better known; whereas if we explain mental things in terms of matter, we are elucidating things inadequately known by means of things less known. Nevertheless the superior *definiteness* of the material world over the mental is a great advantage in favour of the former. There are many things which can be clearly seen from the objective side, which would escape us from the subjective; and a healthy Materialism (side by side with the other view) has its proper and important use, and is by no means to be neglected.

In addition to the debate as to which is prior, Mind or Matter, there is the further controversy as to which, in the constitution of the Mind itself, comes first and is most fundamental—Feeling or Intellect. This question, however, is not quite on all fours with the other. For the question of Mind and Matter is mainly a metaphysical one, as of two possible aspects of Being; whereas the other is rather a question of observation, and of the order of evolution. I think it will become clear to any one who thinks carefully about the question, that notwithstanding a vast amount of interaction between the two, Feeling is more fundamental than Intellect, and prior to it in the order of expression and evolution. Vague desire arises in the mind before ever it takes any form sufficiently definite to be characterised as Thought. This subject, however, I deal with in chap. ii. ("The Art of Creation") more in detail, and I will not dwell upon it here.

What we have just said about the necessity of positing a state of 'Being' prior to Mind (as we use that term) and Matter, indicates to us—and it is necessary to dwell upon this for a moment—that the problem of the Universe *is essentially insoluble to our ordinary thought.* It is necessary to face this fact fairly and squarely, because by blinking it and deceiving ourselves we get landed in hopeless morasses and vain quests. The problem of the Universe is essentially insoluble without the introduction of some transcendent factor—Will, Being, the Ego, a Fourth dimension, or whatever we may term it. The ordinary consciousness, forced to see everything under the double form of subject and object, mind and matter, cannot escape this dual compulsion; and yet at the same time its own constitution compels it to realise and to assume that there is another order of being (unrepresentable in thought) in which the duality is merged in unity. It is thus, as it were by its own action, driven against a wall which it cannot overpass, and forced to set a barrier to its own further progress!

Immensely valuable as is the work which physical Science has done, it suffers from this disability which must be fairly faced, namely, that it never can by any possibility explain the situation, since it moves always on one side of a fixed wall or fence. To pass the fence transcendental things have to be assumed, and that means that at a certain point the ordinary mind must throw up the sponge! The situation would be desperate, were it not that perfectly naturally and inevitably in its due time another order of consciousness opens out, which reconciles subject and object, mind and matter, and having one leg firmly planted on the other side, lifts us gently over the stile!

In the two chapters on "The Self and its Affiliations," I have assumed that the Ego, a transcendental being, descends into and manifests itself in our ordinary world of Time and Space; and that even as the ego of the tiniest cell it has a potential existence far transcending the minute speck of protoplasm which we can actually see or analyse. This may be thought to be an enormous and unwarrantable assumption, but I have given the reason why assumptions of some such kind are unavoidable And it may be pointed out that if, endeavoring to keep to the lines of pure physical science, we barred out such assumptions, we should only be landed in an infinity and an unthinkability of another kind. For to understand and define a single tiniest cell, it is a mere truism of science to say, we should have to understand and define all its environment in space and time, or in other words the whole universe. If therefore we find the subject becomes *more* thinkable by assuming say a fourth dimensional being than by following the ramifications of "matter and force" into infinite space and time, we are quite justified in adopting the former method.

For while we have to admit on the one hand that these problems cannot be fully worked out by ordinary thought, we are bound on the other hand (and we necessarily desire) to make their solutions as thinkable as possible. Thinkable in some degree our views of the world must be (even if not absolutely true), or else we cannot use them in our ordinary lives; and however, in course of time, our ordinary modes of thought may be illuminated by a superior order of consciousness, they will still retain their importance and their value in their own sphere.

To show the limits of ordinary thought and the points where the various problems hand them selves over to other stages of consciousness, is part of the object of this series of papers. It is in these stages of consciousness and their succession (which is a practical matter) that the solution of the great world-problems will, I think, be found. And many of the present riddles of existence, which vex us so, will when we compass the 'cosmic' stage simply be left lying as matters of no importance — not to say left 'lying,' as seen to be the delusive things they are.

II

THE ART OF CREATION[1]

In speaking of "The Art of Creation"—as there may be some ambiguity about the expression—I wish to say that my object is to consider by what process or method things are made to appear and exist in the world. This may seem a bold matter to discuss; but it has, of course, been the subject of philosophy time out of mind.

Forty or fifty years ago the materialistic view of the world was much in evidence. We all at that time were automatons; and it was the fashion to regard human beings as composed of enormous crowds of material atoms, by whose mechanical impacts all human actions were produced, and even certain mental phenomena in the shape of consciousness were evolved as a sort of by-product. Since then, however, partly through a natural reaction and partly through the influx of Eastern ideas, there has been a great swing of the pendulum, and a disposition to posit the Mental world as nearer the basis of existence and to look upon material phenomena rather as the outcome and expression of the mental. In the later part of last century we looked upon

[1] Given originally as an address.

Creation as a process of Machinery; to-day we look upon it as an Art.

But as no theory or view of things in general is of much value unless founded on actual observation in detail, I should like the reader to consider how things we know about actually do come into existence. And since it is best in such cases to observe things that are near us and that we know most about, I propose that we should first consider how our own Thoughts and Actions and Bodily Forms come into existence.

Let us take our Thoughts first. We have only to indulge in a few moments' rest, and immediately we become aware that our mind is peopled by a motley crowd of phantoms. We seem to see them springing up of themselves, and almost at random, from the background of consciousness—images of scenes, the countenances of friends, concatenations of arguments and of events—an innumerable procession. Where does it all come from? Yet a moment more and we see that the crowd is not a random one, but that it is inspired and given its form by the emotions, the feelings, the desires, lying deep and half-hidden within. We are depressed, and the forms and images that pass before us are those of disaster and fear; or we are in high spirits and the scenes are scenes of joy and gladness. This is familiar ground, of course, but it may be worth while considering it more in detail.

Feeling (or desire) lies beneath. Thought is the form which it takes as it comes into the outer world.[1] Let us take a definite instance. We desire to travel. The desire begins first as a mere vague sense of discomfort or restlessness; presently it takes shape as a wish to leave home or to visit other regions. It may remain at that for some time; then it takes somewhat more definite shape—as to go to the seaside. Then we consult our wife, we consider ways and means, we fumble through Bradshaw, the thought of Margate comes as a kind of inspiration, and a quite distinct and clearly formed plan emerges.

Or we wish to build ourselves a house of our own. For a long time this may only be a kind of cloudy pious aspiration. But at last and almost inevitably, the dream of the house takes shape within our minds. We get so far as to make a pencil sketch of what we want. We go

[1] Though there are some who dispute the priority of Feeling, and though undoubtedly there is a great interaction between Feeling and Intellect, so that intellectual states sometimes produce emotional states, and the two are often or even generally intertangled—yet on the whole it is clear, I think, that Feeling is the more fundamental of the two, and prior to Intellect. Ribot ("Psychology of the Emotions") mentions various cases in which emotion appears unaccompanied by any intellection—as in earliest infancy before perceptions are awakened, or in some cases of disease where vague sadness or dread makes its first appearance without taking *any* form or having any apparent reason. He thinks there is an "autonomous life of feeling, independent of the intellectual life, and having its cause below" (p. 9). Paul Deussen points out ("Elements of Metaphysics," p. 113) that desire precedes intellect in infancy and survives it in old age; and Herbert Spencer, in his "Facts and Fragments," p. 27, says "the emotions are the masters, the intellect is the servant." We may also notice that in the order of evolution sensation precedes perception, and that a vegetative nervous system appears in the lower animals long before anything resembling a brain is developed.

and prospect a site. We consult an architect, and presently there emerges a much more definite and detailed plan than before. Then steps are actually taken towards building. Heaps of bricks and stone and other materials begin to appear on the scene; and at last there is the house standing, which once only existed in the dream-world of our minds. Always the movement is outwards, from the indefinite vague Feeling or desire to the definite clearly formed Thought, and thence to Action and the External world.

Whatever feeling it is, the result is the same. We harbour within us the desire to injure any one, or the desire to benefit any one. The desire cannot remain at that stage. It must either perish away, or else if it is harboured it will grow. It will grow into definite thoughts and plans of benefit or of injury. And these thoughts and plans will grow into Actions. True, the actions may not be seen immediately; the thoughts and plans may work unseen for a long time. Still, there they are, working; there they are making ready the channels for action. And this it is, I suppose, which explains the fact that we all of us at times act so much more heroically than either our neighbours, or even ourselves, expect; and also, I am afraid, that at times we act so much more meanly. All the time, in silence, thought has been busy within, making ready the channels; and so one day when a great rush of feeling comes it flows down, and in an instant, as it were, before we have time to say

Yea or Nay, has flung itself forth into our actions, and taken form and standing in the visible world.

And not only is this true of violent feeling, that it finds expression in the visible world; but even of very quiet feeling the same, if it is also Persistent. If so small a creature as man presses with his hand against the side of a great ship floating in dock, it seems that no result is produced; yet we know that if he should continue persistently so to press, in time a measurable effect would ensue. And so it is with those smaller calmer currents of desire and feeling within us. If they are always there, always flowing, they will inevitably show themselves in time. Gradually, insensibly, they modify our thoughts, our actions, our habits of action, the movements of our muscles and limbs, the expressions of our faces, the forms of our bodies. Yes, even the forms of our bodies, the forms and outlines of our faces, our expressions and manners, and the tones of our voices—all the things that go to make up our appearance in the world—are, I will not say entirely the result (since Heredity and other things have to be considered), but plainly to a very great extent the result and expression of those dim feelings and emotions, which, welling up in the hidden caverns of the mind, gradually press forward and outward into the light of day.

So far, then, we seem to come upon something which we may call a Law of Nature, just as much as gravitation or any other law—the law, namely, that within ourselves there is a continual movement outwards from Feeling towards Thought, and then to Action; from the inner to the outer; from the vague to the definite; from the emotional to the practical; from the world of dreams to the world of actual things and what we call reality.

It will be said, however, that though this general movement of feeling and thought towards the outer and 'real' world may truly be noticed, yet there is an immense and everlasting difference between thoughts and actual things—between the sketch of the house in my mind, and the actual house of stone and mortar. The one is a mere dream, an insubstantial phantom inside my brain, which no one but myself can see or feel; the other is a solid and undeniable fact which would crack my skull and my brain both, if they came into too sudden contact with it. Nevertheless, as I have shown that between a man's thoughts and his actions there is no positive line of separation that can be drawn; so I want it to be realised, as we go on, that the house as it exists in the man's brain, and the house as it stands on the hillside, are not two entirely separate things; that an essential unity enfolds them; and that the same Art of Creation which is concerned in the production of one is also concerned in the production of the other.

But first I would say a word about dreams. I have pointed out that in our waking hours continual processions of Thoughts are passing through the mind, stimulated by underlying feeling. In the dreams of sleep we notice the same ebullition of images, only we say, and rightly, that they are more scrappy, more incoherent, more grotesque. The truth is, doubtless, that in sleep the higher reasoning centres of the brain are quiescent, and consequently the growth of images takes place more at random and less harmoniously. But what I want you to notice is that the same rule as before governs, and that the dream-images are, for the most part, inspired or evoked by dim underlying feelings. We go to sleep with insufficient covering on, and immediately dream of plunging through snowdrifts, or falling into a crevasse; or we have eaten a heavy supper, and are haunted by most discomfortable apparitions, which image and represent to us in outward form the discomfort we feel within. That hunger or any other need or desire of the body evokes illustrative dreams is a commonplace remark. A friend of mine in the interior of Africa years ago, with an exploring party, was for eight days without food—nothing but a parrot and a mud-fish having been obtained during that time! He said that one of the worst trials of the starvation was the impossibility of sleep which it brought with it. And when, worn out with fatigue, he did relapse into slumber for a minute or two, it was only to be visited by a most tantalising dream. For at once he beheld what he described as "a most delicious dish of mutton-cutlets" floating towards him. Of course, no sooner did he stretch his hand to seize the prize, than he woke, and the vision departed; but he said that if during those fateful days he dreamed of that blessed dish once, he dreamed of it a hundred times!

Here we see an almost poetic and artistic effort of the slumbering mind to express the underlying desire for food in the most lovely and attractive form which it could devise. And some folk, who are of a literary turn, are not unaccustomed to find themselves composing dream-verses, which are expressive in their way—even if not perfect models of composition. An acquaintance of mine, who was accustomed to keep a pencil and paper by his bedside for such occasions, told me that he once woke in the night feeling himself drenched with a sense of seraphic joy and satisfaction, while at the same time a lovely stanza which he had just dreamed lingered in his mind. Quickly he wrote it down, and immediately fell asleep again. In the morning waking, after a while he bethought himself of the precious experience, and turning to look at the words, which he doubted not would make his name immortal, he read:—

Walker with one eye,
Walker with two,
Something to live for,
And nothing to do.

Here again we find that the deep feeling in which the sleeper's mind was drenched had got so far as to instinctively clothe itself in rhyme and rhythm. This at any rate was an important move in the direction of expression, even though the poetry produced was not of a very high order ! Still, one must feel that the ideal of "something to live for, and nothing to do" was a very blessed and beautiful one in its way !

There is a class of dreams which occur not unfrequently under anæsthetics, which are interesting because they illustrate this expressive symbolic quality. There is good reason to believe that under anæsthetics there is a separation effected between the grosser material body and the more subtle and highly conscious part—a separation from the connection of pain, and a liberation, so to speak, of the inner being. And it is curious that under anæsthetics dreams so frequently occur in which one seems to be flying or soaring through space with a great sense of joy and liberation. I have heard of many instances. The following rather poetic dream was told me by a friend as consequent on the somewhat prosaic operation of having a tooth removed under gas. He dreamed immediately that he was soaring through space with an intense feeling of freedom and ecstasy. Up and up through the ethereal regions he went —till suddenly he popped out on the floor of heaven ! And there (I suppose he had been reading Plato) he beheld the twelve gods seated in a semicircle, and filled (as the gods should be) with inextinguishable joy and laughter. And well might they laugh ; for now he became conscious of himself, there on the floor of heaven, as a small transparent ball of jelly, in the centre of which was a speck, which he knew to be his very self or ego. He also was greatly amused, and was just about to join in the laughter, when he heard behind him a horrible sound, as of the belling of a gigantic bloodhound; and a sense of awful despair seized him as he realised that his body, with its mouth wide open, was in pursuit of him. Escape was hopeless; there was a moment of agony as he was swallowed down; and then he woke up to find his tooth out! In a dream like this, though one cannot suppose it to be an accurate description or vision of what actually took place, yet one may well suppose it to be an artistic representation of real facts and feelings, and an endeavour to portray them in the symbols and images of the world we know.

Thus what I want the reader to notice is that the operation of the mind in dreams is along similar lines to that of our waking hours—though naturally not quite so perfect—that is, it proceeds from underlying feeling to images and thoughts which represent the feeling, and which continually become more distinct and 'real.' [I need hardly say that I am not here giving a complete theory of dreams, for there may be some dreams that fall under other heads; but I am simply citing them in illustration of my principle.]

The tendency is, I say, for all these images evoked in our minds by feeling to grow on us and become more and more distinct and real;

and indeed in dreams we wonder sometimes at the *intense* reality of the images we see. But it is really quite the same in waking life. We are walking down the street on some errand; but presently forgetting about our proper business, the mind wanders away just as in dreamland, and we imagine ourselves talking to some friend in Australia, or at the club arguing violently some question with an opponent. The scene grows more and more distinct, more real to us, we become quite lost in it—till suddenly—we run against the lamp-post! then of course the dream is dissipated. Something *more* real than it has arrived. But in the dreams of sleep there is no lamp-post; and so they go on gathering reality, till they seem as actual to us as the events of the outer world. The chief difference between the thoughts of our waking hours and those of sleep is that the former are constantly *corrected* and set in order by the presence of the actual world around us, whereas the visions of sleep grow undisturbed like plants in a hothouse defended from the winds, or like weeds in a sheltered and neglected corner of the garden.

That this is so, is shown by the fact that our waking thoughts too can gain the same reality as our dreams if they are only encouraged and defended from outer disturbance. When you sit by the fire in the twilight there is little to distract your attention, and your thoughts in such reveries seem strangely real. I have heard of people who indulged in such day-dreams, carrying them on from day to day, retiring to their rooms always at a certain hour, and taking them up where left the day before, till their life spent in this way seemed as real as their ordinary life. And there are other people, Authors of novels, or Dramatists, who deliberately do this—who deliberately isolate themselves and concentrate their minds till the figures and characters so created become like living men and women. And not only to themselves; but to the world at large. So that to-day, to every one of us, there are scores of characters created by the great dramatists and authors, of which it is hard for us at the moment to say whether they are men and women whom we actually remember, or whether they are such creations from books. The truth being that the author with immense labour has projected his own feeling, his own vitality, into figures and forms with such force, that they begin to compete in reality with the figures and forms of the actual world.

We may then, I think, fairly conclude from what has been said that the same process may be witnessed both in our waking thoughts and in our dreams—namely, a continual ebullition and birth going on within us, and an evolution out of the Mind-stuff of forms which are the expression and images of underlying feeling; that these forms, at first vague and undetermined in outline, rapidly gather definition and clearness and materiality, and press forward towards expression in the outer world. And we may fairly ask whether we are not here within our own minds witnessing *what is really the essential process of Creation*, taking place everywhere and at all times—in other persons as well as ourselves, and in the great Life which underlies and is the visible universe.

But it will be said, We can see that the feel ings in Man clothe themselves in mental images, which he, by throwing his vitality more and more into them, can make practically real to himself; and which by roundabout processes like writing books or setting workmen to build houses he can in time body forth and make real to other folk. But ought he not, if your theory be correct, to be able to throw those mental images *direct* into the outer world so as to become visible and tangible to others, at once, and without intermediate operations? To which I answer, *Don't be in too great a hurry.* I believe man *has* the germ of such power, and *will* have it in greater degree. But because he can travel so far along the route at present it does not follow that with his yet undeveloped powers he can at once reach the point of being able to project his thoughts instantly into the world around him.

Yet I would like you in this connection to consider a few facts. In the first place, is it not true that in moments of great feeling there flashes something out of people's faces and figures which *is* visible at once to those around, and which is intensely real, quite as real as a lightning flash, or immovable as a mass of rock? In the second place, has not the modern study of telepathy, by careful and scientific methods, shown pretty conclusively that images can be projected by one mind and be seen or felt by others at a distance? Thirdly, do not the well-established phenomena of Wraiths, or the Ghosts of those in the act of dying, point in the same direction—namely, that in such moments the whole vitality of a person may pour itself out towards a loved one and impress itself powerfully as a real presence on the latter's mind.

There are other considerations connected with what is called Spiritualism, which are very interesting, but which I have not time to dwell on at any length. There seems a mass of evidence to show that in connection with so-called mediums in a state of Trance images are evolved which become visible and even tangible to a small circle of people. Now as we have seen that in Reverie, when one's body is at rest and the world around one is still, one's vitality may go into one's thoughts to such a degree as to render them strangely real; and as in Dreams, when one's body is *asleep*, the images become more real still; so in Trance, which is a still deeper sleep, does it seem quite possible that the inner vitality of the Medium may shape itself into images so far material as to be visible even to other folk. At any rate evidence points in this direction; and the well-known fact that the Medium is often greatly exhausted after these manifestations, corroborates the idea. For since an author who spends three or four hours in writing a novel or a play—thus doing some of the hardest work to which a mortal can devote himself—is all the time throwing out his mental vitality to inspire, embody, and create those images which he gives to the world, and in the process naturally is intensely exhausted; so by a parity of reasoning we should expect that the medium out of whose mind-stuff such images were directly created would be exhausted in even worse fashion.[1] [I may also remind the reader how tiring it is to any one in ordinary sleep to *dream* excessively.]

However, leaving these passing illustrations, I will now proceed along the main line of argument. Whatever we may think about the last few remarks, we do see *within ourselves* a very distinct process in operation. There is the first birth of dim vague Feeling or Desire; then the growth in clearness and intensity of that Feeling; then its shaping into distinct Thoughts or Images; till these latter become intensely real to ourselves; then the descent of Thought and Feeling into our Nerves and Muscles, our Habits and Manners, the expression of our Faces, the very forms of our Bodies; and their ultimate translation into Action, and the results of our actions in the Outer World. Of this process there is no doubt. And thus we see that there is in Man a

1 Here again I am not attempting to give a complete theory of Spiritualism, but only to show how some of its phenomena illustrate the main contention of my lecture.

Creative Thought-source continually in operation, which is shaping and giving form not only to his body, but largely to the world in which he lives. In fact, the houses, the gardens, the streets among which we live, the clothes we wear, the books we read, have been produced from this source. And there is not one of these things—the building in which we are at this moment, the conveyance in which we may ride home—which has not in its first birth been a mere phantom Thought in some man's mind, and owes its existence to that fact. Some of us who live in the midst of what we call Civilisation simply live embedded among the thoughts of other people. We see, hear, and touch those thoughts, and they are, for us, our World.

But no sooner do we arrive at this point, and see the position clearly, than another question inevitably rises upon us. If, namely, this world of civilised life, with its great buildings and bridges and wonderful works of art, is the embodiment and materialisation of the Thoughts of Man, how about that other world of the mountains and the trees and the mighty ocean and the sunset sky—the world of Nature—is that also the embodiment and materialisation of the Thoughts of other Beings, or of one other Being? And when we touch these things are we also coming into touch with the thoughts of these beings?

It may seem rather absurd to some folk to suppose that rocks and stones and trees and waterspouts can be the expression of any one's thoughts. But that does not prove the thing to be impossible. We know that to primitive savages *writing* (so familiar to us) appears just such an impossible thing. Some time ago I heard a well-authenticated story of a trader up-country in a distant land, and among a people utterly unused to civilisation, who had each week to send a basket of provisions to another European who lived some miles away. The native who carried the basket was naturally much tempted by the fowls, bread, eggs, or what other things it contained; and on one occasion, being overcome, took some of the food, then covered up the basket and delivered it as usual. But the man who received it took up a little piece of paper (which of course contained a list of the articles) from the basket, looked at it, and then said, You have taken a loaf and so many eggs. The native, horror-struck, confessed his sin, and was punished. After which he refrained for some time; but at last gave way again—and of course with the same result. He had a great fear of that little bit of paper. He thought it was *fetish*, *tabu*. Not for one instant did it occur to him that those little scratches and dots on it could mean anything, could have any sense. No, he thought the paper was *alive*, and that it *saw* what he did, and told the man. So he determined what to do. The next time he felt hungry, he waited till he came to a lonely spot. Then he put the basket down, took out the bit of paper, not without fear and trembling, carried it off a little distance, and hid it behind a rock, *where it could not see him or the basket.* Then he helped himself freely, and having done so, smoothed the napkin nicely over the top, put the paper back, and delivered the basket as usual. Alas! it was no use. The paper told all. He was punished again, and from that time he abandoned the affair as hopeless.

But if the savage takes a long time to learn that these lines and marks on paper have meaning, may it not also take us a long time to learn that these lines of the sea and sunset sky, these forms and colours of the trees and the flowers, are the expression of ideas waiting perhaps through the ages for their interpreters.

It is curious that we admit intelligence in Man, though we cannot prove it. I am hopeful that you perceive some intelligence in me. But you cannot absolutely *prove* that I feel and think: for all you know I may be merely a cleverly-made automaton. You only *infer* that I feel and think from a comparison of my actions and movements with your own. And so, on the same grounds, we infer intelligence in dogs and monkeys, because their movements still resemble ours in some degree. [But we must remember that Descartes and other philosophers have contended that animals *were* merely machines or automata without feeling; and certainly one is almost obliged to think that some of our vivisecting Professors adopt the same view.] When, however, we come to creatures whose movements do *not* much resemble ours, like worms and oysters and trees, it is noticeable that we become very doubtful as to whether they feel or are conscious, and even disinclined to admit that they are. Yet it is obviously only a question of degree; and if we allow intelligence in our fellow men and women, and then in dogs, horses, and so forth, where and at what particular point are we to draw the line? In fact, it is obvious that the main reason why we do not allow intelligence in an oyster is because we do not understand and interpret its movements as well as we do those of a dog. But it is quite conceivable that to one of its own kind another oyster may appear the most lovely and intelligent being in creation.

Certainly it is quite probable that the feeling and consciousness in an oyster or a tree is different and less extended than in a man or a dog; but that in its order and degree it is quite as intense and definite I hardly doubt.

What is it that before all convinces us that there is an intelligent Self in our fellow-man? It is that he has a Will and Purpose, a *Character*, which, do what you will, tends to push outwards towards Expression. You put George Fox in prison, you flog and persecute him, but the moment he has a chance he goes and preaches just as before. And so with all of us. Our lives, despite all the blows of fortune and misfortune, spring again and again from a mental root which we recognise as our real selves: which we want to express, which we must express, and to express which is our very life. But take a Tree, and you notice exactly the same thing. A dominant Idea informs the life of the Tree; persisting, it *forms* the tree. You may snip the leaves as much as you like to a certain pattern, but they will only grow in their own shape. You may cut off a branch, and another will take its place. You may remove a small twig, and even that twig will have within it the pervading character or purpose, for if you plant it in the ground, another tree of the same shape will spring from it. Finally, you may cut the tree down root and branch, and burn it, but if there is left a single seed, within that seed in an almost invisible point lurks the formative ideal, which under proper conditions will again spring into life and expression.

I need hardly remind you here how exactly similar to that seed, is the little compressed Desire or Need which at the very beginning of this argument we saw, as it were, lurking in the human breast, and which afterwards, under the proper conditions, grew out into a House or some other great objective result in the external world. Look at the huge network of Railways, now like an immense Tree, with endless branches encircling the globe. Once that Tree slept in the form of a little compressed Thought or feeling in the breast of George Stephenson, the collier-lad, and unbeknown and invisible to any but himself.

And now, at this time of year, there are lying and being buried in the great Earth thousands and thousands of millions of seeds of all kinds of plants and trees, which during the long winter will slumber there like little dream-images in the brain of the great globe, waiting for their awakening.[1] And when the Spring comes with the needful conditions, they will push forward towards their expression and materialisation in the outer world, even as every thought presses towards its manifestation in us.

Thus, as we think about it, it becomes more and more possible to see that this solid earth, and the great liquid sea, and even the midnight sky with its wonderful starry systems which from dream-like nebulæ have gradually through the ages cohered into definite and one may say living organisms—that this great world of Nature, just as much as the world of Man, is the panorama of a conscious life ever pressing forward towards Expression and Manifestation; and that these dots and scratches in the writing, these stones and stars and storms, are words appealing to us continually for our loving understanding and interpretation. We conclude the intelligence of our friends because we should find it absurd and impossible to place ourselves on a lonely pinnacle and look upon those we love as automatons.

[1] Who knows but what our brains in the same way are full of tiny atoms—seed-atoms of desire and purpose—which lie there silent and compressed, till conditions liberate them to long trains of action in the drama of humanity?

And in the same way, in proportion as we come to love and understand the animals and the trees and the face of Nature shall we find it impossible to deny intelligence to these. Certainly there are times, as for instance in looking at some beautiful landscape or sunset sky, when not only we seem to perceive, as the Greeks did, separate presences or spirits in the trees and the plants and the streams, but we seem to feel the overshadowing of a universal Mind—"A sense sublime," as Wordsworth has it,

> "Of something far more deeply interfused,
> Whose dwelling is the light of setting suns,
> And the round ocean, and the living air,
> And the blue sky, and in the mind of man—
> A motion and a spirit that impels
> All thinking things, all objects of all thought,
> And rolls thro' all things."

Creation, then, is not an almighty *fiat*, by which things are suddenly out of nothing given form and solidity—or if it is, it is a process of which we have no experience, and which is unintelligible to us. On the other hand we cannot regard it as a fortuitous concourse of material atoms, because we have no experience of such atoms or of their existence; and if Creation were such a concourse of senseless things, it would be itself senseless and mere nonsense (which it certainly is not). But it is a process, I take it, which we can see at any time going on within our own minds and bodies, by which forms are continually being generated from feeling and desire; and, gradually acquiring more and more definition, pass outward from the subtle and invisible into the concrete and tangible. This process, I say, we can observe within ourselves in the passage from Emotion to Thought, and from these again to Action and the External world. It is the foundation of all human Art. The painter, the sculptor, the musician are for ever bringing their dreams of Beauty and Perfection forward from the most intimate recesses and treasure-houses of their hearts and giving them a place in the world. And not only the Artist and Musician, but every workman who makes things does the same The world of Man is created by this process; and I have given reasons for supposing that the world of Nature is continuous with that of man, and that there too innumerable Beings are for ever labouring to express themselves, and so to enter into touch and communication with each other.

[The reader may say there is no evidence that man ever produces a particle of matter directly out of himself; and I will admit that is so. But there is plenty of evidence that he produces shapes and forms, and if he produces shapes and forms that is all we need; for what matter is in the abstract no one has the least experience or knowledge. All we know is that the things we see are shapes and forms of what we *call* matter. And if (as is possible and indeed probable) Matter is of the same stuff as Mind—only seen and envisaged from the opposite side—then the shapes and forms of the actual world are the shapes and forms of innumerable Minds, our own and others, thus projected for us mutually to witness and to understand. However, there I leave the argument.]

I will only, in conclusion, say that in this view Creation is a stupendous and perpetually renewed work of Art, an everlasting evolution and expression of inner meanings into outer form,[1] not only in the great whole, but in every tiniest part; Nature is a great vehicle, an innumerable network and channel of intelligence and emotion; and this whole domain of the universe the theatre of an immense interchange of conscious life. Countless hosts of living beings, of every grade of organisation and consciousness, are giving utterance to themselves, expressing and unfolding that which is within them—even as every child of man from birth to death is constantly endeavouring to express and unfold and give utterance to what lies within him. With incredible speed the messages of these intelligences flash through space; "the Morning Stars sing together"; the messages of light and sound and electricity and attraction penetrate everywhere; and as modern science shows us that the air, the sea, and the solid frame of the earth itself may be the vehicle of waves which without wire or definite channel may yet convey our thoughts safely to one another

[1] I have in this paper dwelt only on this one aspect of the World and Existence—that of its movement outwards—its generation and birth. There is of course and necessarily, an opposite aspect of equal importance—that of its absorption and involution from the outer to the inner.

through intervening leagues of distance, so surely we must believe that the countless vibrations ever going on around, and ever radiating from and impinging on every known object, are messengers too of endless meaning and feeling.

The intelligences which constitute the universe are doubtless of infinite variety and of infinite gradation in development. Some may find expression in a mere point of space, others may enclose a planet or a solar system. Some are harmonious and accordant together; others may be—as we well know—in violent mutual hostility or warfare. Yet in the end they are included. To regard the world as simply an arena of separate warring beings and personalities is impossible, because (as all Science, Philosophy, and Experience convince us) there is inevitably a vast unity underlying all; and all these beings and personalities must root down in one ultimate Life and Intelligence; all of them in the end and deep down must have a common purpose and object of existence—and in that thought there is liberation, in that thought there is rest.

III

MATTER AND CONSCIOUSNESS

THE world consists of what is (or can be) known or perceived. There is no other world obviously that we know or can know anything about.

But what is this act of knowing, which is so important?

Every act of knowing involves three aspects, which we cannot avoid, and under which (by the present nature of our minds) we are forced to regard it. There is (1) the knower or perceiver, (2) the knowledge or perception, (3) the thing to be known or perceived. I say we cannot imagine the act of knowledge or perception except in this triple form.

For the first analysis of the conception of knowledge implies and compels the thought of a knower—either oneself or some one else. If it is our own knowledge, then we cannot avoid the thought of self as the knower; if it is knowledge in some far planet, totally beyond our sphere, still we are forced to think of it as entertained by some being, be it beetle or angel, who is thus the knower. And without some knower the conception of knowledge is (to us) meaningless.[1]

Similarly the act of knowledge at first analysis yields a "thing to be known";—we cannot avoid thinking there is something of which we have the knowledge or perception. If an impression is made on our mind the very word connotes, as Herbert Spencer says, "something that impresses as well as something that is impressed," or, in other words, the "modification of our mind" which we call knowledge compels us to look for something which *causes* the modification. We are startled by a thunder-clap; instantly we ask, What *is* the thunder, what is behind it? We are told that it is Zeus, or God, or Electricity. The answers do not bring us much further, but they indicate the conviction that there is "something." This habit of the mind of positing a something behind and different from the knowledge itself may be foolish, but it is apparently quite inveterate and unavoidable. Though we do not seem able to say *what* the "thing known" is, we seem to see quite clearly that is *not* the knowledge. Here is a violet.

[1] Thus J. F. Ferrier in his "Institutes of Metaphysics" gives it as his first and foundation proposition that "Along with whatever any intelligence knows it must, as the ground or condition of its knowledge, have some cognisance of *itself*"; and later, "The objective and the subjective part do together constitute the unit or *minimum* of knowledge." Sir William Hamilton also says, "In the act of perception Consciousness gives us a conjoint fact, an Ego or mind, and a Non-Ego or matter, known together and contradistinguished from each other." Some modern psychologists have endeavoured to impugn this view, but not very successfully. (See note, p. 70, chap. v.)

The least thought shows us that the colour of the flower is largely in our own sensations. The same of its odour. We know that such colours and smells appeal differently to different eyes and noses. What then is the violet "in itself"? We do not know; we are tempted to say that it certainly is *not* the violet that we see and smell. Yet we are compelled to believe that there is an entity there. And in all our knowledge and perception, whatever it may be, we cannot get over this ascription of an Objective side to it, as well as of a Subjective. Even in our dreams, those most tenuous phantoms, we are oppressed with a sense of their "reality."

The distinction of Subject and Object is fundamental in our minds (as at present constituted). Practically all the philosophers agree in this—and there are not many things that they do agree about. All our knowledge implies and involves these two aspects. There is always an Ego side to it, and always a Non-Ego side. Consciousness—to use the simile of Ferrier—is like a stick. It has two ends, and without the two ends we cannot imagine it. All knowledge, be it great or small, simple or complex, has two poles, the subject and the object. The least atom of the knowledge (as in a magnet) has the same constitution. All our knowledge is saturated and interpenetrated by the union and distinction of subject and object. And we are compelled to think it so.[1]

[1] Kant's doctrine of *Causality* as a necessary form of the understanding comes to the same thing. The experience,

Nevertheless, it need hardly be said, this analysis, in young children, animals, and very primitive folk, scarcely takes place. The knower, the knowledge, and the thing known are in experience undistinguished, darkly confused together, as it were one; the Ego quite dim, only now and then, so to speak, *suspected;* the thing to be known and the knowledge frankly unseparated. This may be called the state of simple consciousness. Yet again *we*, considering it, are compelled, if we believe there is knowledge, to believe also there is a Knower and a Known, an ego side and an object side—even though these sides, in the simple consciousness, have not yet become separated.

Once then the Nature of knowledge, as above indicated, is seized, many things easily follow.

In the first place, it is obvious that Matter, *per se*, as an independent entity supposed apart from some act of knowledge, is absolutely unknown to us. Matter, of course, is a general and in its way useful term for the supposed objective entity underlying phenomena and our sensations. I say that to figure this entity as independent and apart from mind is impossible. For knowledge is the subject *plus* the object, the object *plus* the subject. It is, and always must be, relative in some degree to the Subject or Ego. Something therefore *not* relative to any ego or subject, but having an

whatever it is, is at once conceived as having a cause; and this cause is projected into space, as the object. Thus subject *plus* object is the necessary form of Thought.

independent non-mental existence of its own, cannot be known. It cannot even be imagined. The instrument or act of knowledge being itself partly subjective can only at best give us information of some joint relation between self and the supposed external entity; and if the "thing outside" can exist without relation to any self or ego, all knowledge is absolutely silent about it. If there is an objective and material "violet" existing independent of any conscious mind (either its own or any other), we know and can know nothing whatever about it.[1]

It follows, therefore, that all the talk about a mechanical structure of the universe—as of dead 'matter,' which, apart from any kind of consciousness, moves in obedience to laws of its own; and all the talk about senseless atoms which fly and spin and collide and rebound, and so by unwitting mechanical or chemical processes build up the world we see, is itself senseless, and may be at once dismissed, not only as having no meaning, but as being *incapable* of meaning to us. We cannot think such matter or such atoms, and the

[1] "Some truths there are," says Berkeley, "so near and obvious to the mind, that a man need only open his eyes to see them. Such I take this important one to be, to wit, that all the choir of heaven and furniture of the earth, in a word, all those bodies which compose the mighty frame of the world, have not any subsistence without mind; that their being is, to be perceived or known; that consequently so long as they are not actually perceived by me, or do not exist in my mind, or that of any other created spirit, they must either have no existence at all, or else subsist in the mind of some eternal spirit."

more we try the more we see our inability. Atoms there may be; but if we are to think them, we must think them as related to Mind—either as being centres of consciousness themselves, or as being outlying elements (thoughts) in wider systems of consciousness. We may, of course, think them as being our own thoughts about an unknown objective world (which no doubt they to a large extent are); or again, we may think them as thoughts conveyed to us by another mind or minds (in which case the objective world is conceived of as mental in character). But as 'matter' which might conceivably remain and pursue its course even in a world from which intelligence had departed, we cannot think them.

Again, as "dead Matter" is nonsense, so is another term, lately much used, namely, "unconscious Thought." The very expression is of course self-contradictory. If there is thought, there is consciousness—of some kind; we cannot imagine it otherwise. In strict language the expression is nonsense. But loosely we know that it is used to indicate that in sleep and at other times processes resembling thought seem to go on (either in portions of our minds or bodies or elsewhere), of which we have no consciousness or memory, but of which we use the results. Now, of this there may be two interpretations: either we may suppose conscious thought (in a strict sense—*i.e.* conscious to our own or to some other self) to be really going on in the region indicated; or we may suppose (and this is the view I think most generally entertained) that non-conscious cerebral, mechanical, and chemical changes are taking place which simply turn out at last a result translatable, and so made use of, as conscious thought.

Now the latter supposition we must dismiss; for we have already seen that non-conscious mechanical and chemical actions convey no meaning to our minds and are really inconceivable. We are therefore compelled to adopt the former supposition, namely, that "unconscious Thought" is really conscious thought of some kind, but inherent in or related to another self than our own. And anyhow it is far simpler, and more natural and intelligent, to suppose this than to call in by way of explanation a mechanical non-conscious process which, when we come to look into it, proves meaningless and unimaginable to us, and therefore to be no explanation at all.

In the third place, from the Nature of knowledge it follows that, like Matter, the Ego, *per se*, as an independent entity supposed apart from some act or possible act of knowledge, cannot be even conceived to exist. For the knower, the knowledge, and the known are one from the beginning; and though the one differentiates into three aspects, we cannot *separate* these aspects. The stick has two ends, but we cannot separate the end from the stick. And if we could, what satisfaction were it to have an end without a stick?

Of the Ego we *have* a consciousness, but only in the act of perception or knowledge (which at the same moment involves the consciousness of the Non-Ego). When there is no act of knowledge, there is no consciousness of the Ego. [But, as we shall presently see, when the knowledge becomes perfect knowledge, then the consciousness of the Self also becomes complete.] We cannot be conscious of our ego as unrelated and independent; for consciousness (in the ordinary sense) of course means relation.

This consciousness of the ego, present in the act of knowledge, gradually evolves, as we have seen, and becomes distinct; indeed, it becomes to us the most real thing in the world. It pursues us everywhere; we refer everything to it. Yet it remains curiously simple and unanalysable. We cannot avoid it; but we cannot analyse it, for the simple reason that as soon as it is envisaged *it* becomes the Object, and the real Ego is found to be again at the hither end of the stick. This action is very curious. However intimate the Thought one may entertain, the Ego is instantly beneath it, and *more* intimate—suggesting the idea that it (the ego) is a kind of widely-diffused substance of Mind, of which thoughts are modifications. Indeed, the idea is suggested that possibly all egos are in essence the same—that they are portions or branches of one universal mind-stuff, of which *all* thoughts and existences are modifications.

However, leaving these last considerations aside

for the moment, we see this curious fact, that while we *feel* the ego as a simple unity, we are compelled to *think* it (if we think of it at all) as enormously complex, or, at least, as having the potentiality of enormous complexity. For obviously the self which entertains or is related to all our knowledge and experience cannot be less complex, or have less potentiality of complexity, than the knowledge and experience to which it is related. Consequently, the self appears at once as a simple monad, and an infinite complexity of possible relations.

In the fourth place, having cleared the ground somewhat, the question arises, Are we now in a position to get a clearer idea of the Non-Ego or of 'Matter'? If we have some conception of the nature of the ego (as we are compelled to conceive it), does that throw any light on the nature of the non-ego?

If the ego is impressed, what is that unknown thing which impresses it? or, If the ego enters into relation, what is that correlative unknown thing which enters into relation with it? or, to put it in the plural, In a world of egos capable of entering into relation, what are the correlative Objects? But since there is no such thing as dead Matter, the only answer we can *think* is: the objects are other egos. The egos enter into *relation with each other.*

I say we cannot think otherwise, for we have nothing to place at the other end of the stick, except something similar to what we have at the hither end. We know of nothing else. In all our experience the self and its knowledge are the only things we know of. We may not be right in our surmise, but if we think at all, we are compelled to think thus. There is a certain *probability*, besides, that one end of the stick is similar to the other. If Subject and Object are correlative, as we are forced to think them, then it is hard not to suppose the object similar in nature to the subject. We conceive the subject as a self or intelligence which is one and yet infinitely complex—and it is difficult not to conceive of the correlated object or objects as one or many similar selves—one and yet infinitely complex—the kind of thing which physical science, along its own ways, is constantly searching for and assuming to exist.

Thus, as in the last chapter, we arrive at the conclusion that Knowledge, Perception, Con sciousness[1] are messages or modes of communi cation between various selves—words as it were by which intelligences come to expression, and become known to each other and themselves. All Nature—all the actual world, as known to us or any being—we have to conceive as the countless interchange of communication between countless selves; or, if these selves are really identical, and the one Ego underlies *all* thought and knowledge, then the Subject and Object are the same, and the World, the whole Creation, is Self-revealment.

[1] In its ordinary form.

In these few remarks on Matter and Consciousness generally I have endeavoured to set out not so much what *is*, as what we are compelled to think, as this indeed seems the safer thing to do. How far what we are compelled to think may be taken as evidence of what *is*, is another question, which I will not tackle, but which the philosophers deal with. I will only quote the following remark of J. F. Ferrier's, from the Ontology section of his "Institutes of Metaphysics": "No Existence at all can be conceived by any intelligence anterior to, and aloof from, knowledge. Knowledge of existence—the apprehension of oneself and other things—is alone true existence. This is itself the First, the Bottom, the Origin—and this is what all intelligence is prevented by the laws of reason from ever getting beyond or below."

IV

THE THREE STAGES OF CONSCIOUSNESS

OBSERVATION of the actual facts of life seems to show us pretty distinctly that there are three stages or degrees of Consciousness; and a consideration of the nature of knowledge, as set out in the foregoing paper, would tend to make us expect such three stages.

There is first the stage of Simple Consciousness, in which the knower, the knowledge, and the thing known are still undifferentiated.

Though we cannot observe this directly, nor draw the exact line at which it begins or ceases, we seem to be able to discern its existence clearly enough in the animals. The thought of self as the knower has not arisen upon them, except in low degree and in a few cases; and certainly the thought of the object as distinguishable from the knowledge or perception of it has not arisen. It is the same with very young children and some primitive men. And this non-differentiation of the self in consciousness explains in these cases various facts which are puzzling to us. The horse in the field stands out, patient and placid, through hours or days of cold and rain, simply because not having a distinct consciousness of self, it cannot pity itself. It feels discomfort no doubt; it may feel pain; but it does not project itself and think with dismay that itself will be feeling this discomfort, this pain, to-morrow. Small babies have little fear, for the same reason. [Nevertheless, Fear in the higher animals and young children—apart from a mere instinct of escape—is there, and often very strongly; and this shows us that the consciousness of self *is* dimly beginning. Fear, in fact, is an inevitable accompaniment and means of the evolution of that consciousness; it is the midwife of a birth which in the far past of the human race has accomplished itself with much suffering.]

The knowledge and perception of animals, therefore, owing to this non-differentiation, and owing to the absence of certain causes of dislocation and trouble, is extraordinarily perfect and untampered. It is from the first a part of Nature, and has a cosmic universal quality about it. Their knowledge is, as it were, embedded in the great living intelligent whole (of the world), and therefore each special act of knowledge or perception carries with it a kind of *aura* or diffused consciousness extending far, far around it. We are aware of this *aura* or "fringe" of consciousness in ourselves, and the modern psychologists have dwelt much on it Seton Thompson, in his "Wild Animals I have Known," speaks of them as being "guided by a knowledge that is beyond us"; and in his description of the wild horse which "in spite of all reasons to take its usual path" came along another and so avoided the pitfall set for it, he says, "What sleepless angel is it watches over and cares for the wild animals?" and again, "But the Angel of the wild things was with him, and that incomprehensible warning came." This daemonic or quasi-divine knowledge is—as we shall see—largely lost in the second stage of consciousness, but restored again in the third.

The second stage is that in which the great mass of humanity at present is; it is that in which the differentiation of knower, knowledge, and thing known has fairly set in.

The consciousness of Self becomes more and more distinct, and with it the consciousness of an object antagonising the Self. Some folk say they remember the moment when, as quite young children, to them with a sense of alarm self-consciousness suddenly came. They were suddenly terrified at the thought of self, as of a separate item or atom in this vast world. Whether suddenly or gradually, this feeling of course has come to every one. Its arrival can generally be noticed without difficulty in any young child. It is the beginning of a new era in its development, and from that moment life begins to shape round the self.

But at the same moment, or very shortly after, the child begins to recognise the self in others—in its mother and those around. And—what is curious and interesting—the child ascribes 'selves' also to toys, stones, and what we call inanimate things. In fact, simultaneously with the appearance of the subject in consciousness comes the appearance of the object in consciousness. It is curious that at these early stages the object of knowledge and the knowledge should be differentiated from each other, or begin to be differentiated; but it is so. The child feels not only (as we do) that there is a personality behind the appearance of its mother, but that there is something behind these stocks and stones, and personifies them also. So does the savage. It is the period of fetishism, which correlates with and accompanies the first evolution of the idea of self.[1] And in very truth, feeble and inadequate as this 'anthropomorphism' may be, it will be seen (from what has already been said) that the child, in this respect, is wiser than the man, that its view is really more logical and rational than that of the 'practical' person who contends that the stocks and stones are the real objects, or who posits, in order to explain them, an ultimate 'matter' devoid of intelligence. Anthropomorphism is inevitable to us (in this second stage), and much the best we can do is frankly to accept it.

Such then is the first birth of self-consciousness. But as the evolution of the idea of self goes on, there comes at last a kind of fatal

[1] Later, as the consciousness of the ego evolves, and deepens and lifts, so does the form in consciousness of the object; and the fetish-beings become gods; and the gods rise to greater nobility and majesty.

split between it and the objective side of things. The kindly beliefs of early peoples in beings similar to themselves moving behind and inspiring natural phenomena, and the consequent sense of community of life with Nature, fade away. The subject and object of knowledge drift farther and farther apart. The self is left face to face with a dead and senseless world. Its own importance seems to increase out of all reason; and with the growth of this illusion (for it is an illusion) the knowledge itself becomes dislocated from its proper bearings, becomes cracked and impotent, and loses its former unity with Nature. Objects are soon looked upon as important only in so far as they minister to the (illusive) self; and there sets in the stage of Civilisation, when self-consciousness becomes almost a disease; when the desire of acquiring and grasping objects, or of enslaving men and animals, in order to minister to the self, becomes one of the main motives of life; and when, owing to this deep fundamental division in human nature and consciousness, men's minds are tormented with the sense of sin, and their bodies with a myriad forms of disease.

Physiologically, this period is marked by the growth of the Brain. In animals the cerebrum is small; the great sympathetic system of nerves and the cerebro-spinal system are relatively large. The cerebrum is only, as it were, a small organ attached to these systems to subserve their needs. But the growth of the intellect is at first stimulated by the growth of the 'self' and its needs.

And in man the cerebral portion of the brain, as specially the seat of self-regarding relations, rises into immense importance; and over a long period lapses into a kind of conflict with the great sympathetic system—which, without doubt, is the great organ of the emotions. The emotions and the intellect of man for a long period are at variance, and distress and grief ensue in the mind, as (owing to the organic disharmony) pain and disease prevail in the body.

Finally, with the complete antagonism of subject and object, of 'self' and 'matter,' and all the antagonisms which follow in its wake—of intellect and emotion, the individual and society, and so forth—and the terrible disruptions of life and society which ensue—comes the third stage.

When the illusion of separation is complete and the man has sounded the depths of grief and pain which accompany this illusion, then, one day, often suddenly, the third form of Consciousness dawns, or flashes, upon him—that which has been called the Cosmic, or universal, Consciousness. The object suddenly is seen, is *felt*, to be one with the self. The reconciliation is effected. The long process of differentiation comes to an end, and reintegration takes its place. The knower, the knowledge, and the thing known are once more one—"Objects turn round upon themselves with an exceedingly innocent air, but are visibly not the same."

This form of Consciousness is the only true knowledge—it is the only true existence. And it is a matter of experience; it has been testified to in all parts of the world and in all ages of history. There is a consciousness in which the subject and the object are felt, are *known*, to be united and one—in which the Self is felt to *be* the object perceived ("I *am* the hounded slave"), or at least in which the subject and the object are felt to be parts of the same being, of the same including Self of all. And it is the only true knowledge; for we saw at the beginning that the knower and the thing known are aspects of the act of knowledge, implicit in it, and not to be separated from it—(the knower without the knowledge, or the thing known without the knowledge, being both unthinkable). Therefore they are really one in the knowledge; and though a differentiation takes place in consciousness (thus immensely enriching the knowledge), yet as soon as ever it becomes a *separation*, and the subject and object are thought of as isolated things, (separate 'selves' and 'atoms,' for example), it has already passed over into a sphere of illusion and folly, and has become nonsense. The true knowledge, therefore, is that in which the subject and object are known as one; and is of course a much higher and more perfect form of knowledge than that first—as in the animals—when subject and object *are* one, but never having been distinguished are not known as one.

When this consciousness comes it brings with it a strange illumination. For the object and the ego are felt to be one, not only through the special act of knowledge which unites them, but deep down in their very essence. A circle is, as it were, completed; and the external act of knowledge is no longer merely external, but is transformed into a symbol of a vast underlying life. The *aura*, in fact, of the animals returns with greatly increased intensity: to such a degree, we may perhaps say, that *it* becomes the main thing, and the object or external experience is only of importance as waking it. It is not merely that the object is seen by the eye or touched by the hand, but it is felt at the same instant from within as a *part* of the ego; and this seeing and touching wake an infinite response—a reverberation through all the chambers of being—such as was impossible before. The knowledge, in fact, loses its tentative illusive form of *thought*, and acquires a cosmic universal character. It becomes luminous with far-reaching interpretations.

How shall we denote or explain these things? It is obvious that mere thought (belonging to the second stage of consciousness) does not and can not possibly cover them—any more than a man can walk a square mile. Thought can and does bring us to the edge of the third stage, and within sight, as it were, of the essential facts of the universe; and its value, in that respect alone, is immense; but, like the mule at the edge of the glacier, there is a point where, from the nature of the case, it has to be left behind. We cannot obviously *prove* the ultimate constitution of things. But that which the third order of consciousness conveys, we can illustrate and symbolise in thought.

To illustrate the two orders of consciousness we may, for instance, figure a tree—in which two leaves observe each other externally for a long enough time, mutually exclusive, and without any suspicion that they have a life in common. Then the 'self' consciousness of one of the leaves deepening inwardly (down the twig or branch), at last reaches the point whence the 'self' of the other leaf also branches off—and becomes aware of its unity with the other. Instantly its external observation of its fellow-leaf is transformed; it sees a thousand meanings in it which it never saw before. Its fellow-leaf is almost as much an expression of self as itself is; for both now belong to a larger self—that of the spray or branch from which they depend.

Or when two strangers, of different race and tongue perhaps, meet, they eye each other with suspicion and misunderstanding, and seem to catch only at the most external knowledge of each other—to notice the slant of the brow or the cut of the clothes. But when two folk know each other in the sense of *love* (love being a consciousness of the third kind), instantly a word or a glance of the eyes, in the external world, reveal abysmal depths in the two selves, and a sense of age-long union. Without the external knowledge the two could not know either themselves or the other person (since, as we have seen, the self without the knowledge is unthinkable);

but in the second case the knowledge is transformed, and reveals meanings and depths of the self unimagined before.

In the case of two persons the transformation of knowledge in the third stage of consciousness is easy to understand, since here the so-called subject and object are commonly recognised to be of the same nature, and to have some degree of identity. But in the case of a man observing, say, a tree, we find it more difficult. Yet in truth the process appears to be quite similar. Some people, like Jacob Boehme, the mystic, have been conscious of the hidden qualities of plants and trees they looked on;[1] and innumerable instances of 'second-sight,' well authenticated, must convince us that, in cases, the direct external act of perception brings with it far outlying and underlying tracts of knowledge and illumination. The external knowledge is transformed by being brought into relation with the original source of knowledge, *i.e.* the unity of all beings. It is, in fact, that hidden knowledge realised and made external. To borrow a simile from electricity, the luminous arc springs into being when the circuit is complete, and is the evidence and manifestation of that completeness.

This third mode of consciousness is, I say, the only perfect knowledge; for the first mode (though nearer to the third than the second is) is merely inchoate; while the second mode is sheer

[1] And it is probable that many primitive folk, as well as animals, have, on an inferior plane, intuitions of the same kind.

illusion. It, the second mode, is all built upon the separation of the self from the knowledge and from the object (*i.e.* from other selves). It is therefore built upon an illusion, and is itself illusion. Its form is not true knowledge, but *Thought*. Thought is an aspect; it is the last disintegration of knowledge. It is the fact seen from just one most particular and separate point of view. The (hidden) fact being the unity of my 'self' with that of the tree, all my *thought* about the tree is an attempt to get at that fact from ever-shifting, ever-countless sides; but remains profitless, barren, productive of little but unrest and disappointment—till the moment when the reintegration takes place, subject and object close in one, and the innumerable thoughts fusing in the intense heat of union lose their separateness, and merge in perfect light.

Herbert Spencer touches this point with a kind of unwilling illumination when, speaking of the impossibility of knowing the "substance of Mind," he says,[1] "A thing cannot at the same instant be both subject and object of Thought; and yet the substance of Mind must be this before it can be known." Certainly, a thing cannot at once be subject and object of *thought*, *i.e.* of the second stage of consciousness; because this stage is built on the separation and antagonism of subject and object. But that a thing may be subject and object of the third stage experience shows; and the 'thing' that thus becomes both subject and

1 "Psychology," i. p. 148.

object is the 'self' (which corresponds to Spencer's "substance of Mind"). Thus we conclude that the self or substance of Mind (though it cannot be known in the second stage) may or *must* be known in the third stage of consciousness; and indeed that this is the only way in which it can be known.

Of the existence of this third form of consciousness there is evidence all down History; and witnesses, far removed from each other in time and space and race and language, and perfectly unaware of each other's utterances, agree so remarkably in their testimony, that there is left no doubt that the experience is as much a matter of fact as any other human experience—though the capacity for it is of course not universal. The authors of that extraordinary series of writings, the Upanishads, founded evidently the whole of their teaching on this experience. Their object in the teaching was to introduce others to the same knowledge:—

"He who beholds all beings in the Self, and the Self in all beings, he never turns away from it."

"When to a man who understands, the Self has become all things, what sorrow, what trouble, can there be to him who once beheld that unity?"

"*Tat tvam asi*, Thou art that, Thou art that," says his father to Svetaketu, pointing to object after object, and trying to make him feel that the subtle essence of all these things is his true Self.

"Knowledge has three degrees," says Plotinus—"opinion, science, illumination. . . . It [the last] is absolute knowledge founded on the *identity of the mind knowing with the object known*."

"God is the soul of all things," says Eckhardt, "He is the light that shines in us when the veil [of division] is rent."

Whitman speaks of the light that came to him:—

> "Light rare, untellable, lighting the very light,
> Beyond all signs, descriptions, languages,"

and says—

> "Strange and true, that paradox hard I give,
> Objects gross and the unseen soul are one."

And Tennyson, in a well-known passage, distinguishing the ordinary knowledge from the other, says:—

> "For Knowledge is the swallow on the lake
> That sees and stirs the surface-shadow there
> But never yet hath dipt into the abysm,
> The Abysm of all Abysms, beneath, within
> The blue of sky and sea, the green of earth,
> And in the million-millionth of a grain
> Which cleft and cleft again for evermore,
> And ever vanishing, never vanishes
> And more, my son! for more than once when I
> Sat all alone, revolving in myself
> That word which is the symbol of myself,
> The mortal limit of the Self was loosed,
> And past into the Nameless, as a cloud
> Melts into Heaven. I touched my limbs, the limbs
> Were strange not mine—and *yet no shadow of doubt*,

> *But utter clearness*, and through loss of Self
> The gain of such large life as matched with ours
> Were Sun to spark, unshadowable in words,
> Themselves but shadows of a shadow-world."

And so on.[1] But it is not only the great prophets and seers who prove to us the existence of another stage of consciousness. For to almost all mankind flashes (or glimmers) of the same thing come in those moments of exaltation or intuition which form the basis of religion, art, literature, and much even of practical life. Schopenhauer, who has written well on Art and Music, says that Art and the sense of Beauty give us the most real knowledge of things, because then we see the object as the "realisation of an Idea" (*i.e.* as a form, according to him, of the world-soul); and the beholder (who has the same world-soul within himself) "becomes the clear mirror of the object," and "the distinction of the subject and object vanishes." And every one, whether he agrees with Schopenhauer or not, must have felt in poetry, music, and art generally, and in all cases where the sense of Beauty is deeply roused, that strange impression of passing into another world of consciousness, where meanings pour in and illuminate the soul, and the "distinction between subject and object" vanishes.

[1] Dr. R. M. Bucke in his great work on "Cosmic Consciousness" (Philadelphia, 1901) has gathered together the utterances of a vast number of witnesses, and shown very convincingly their remarkable agreement as to the nature of this consciousness. His prefatory essay on its evolution is also instructive.

The evidence, I say, for the existence of this third stage of consciousness is ample and convincing; and though to do the subject justice would require a volume, yet we can see even from what has already been said that this cosmic sense is perfectly normal and in the line of human progress, and that it surpasses the ordinary consciousness of the second stage as far indeed as that surpasses the first.

It is indeed, from its very nature, as already explained (*i.e.* union of subject and object), the only true and absolute knowledge, and this view of it is corroborated by the testimony of those who have experienced it. It is also the only true *existence* (at least that we can imagine), for, as we have seen, the world consists of what is known, *i.e.* of what enters into consciousness. Consciousness *is* existence; and the perfect consciousness is the perfect and true existence. That universal consciousness by and in which the subject knows itself absolutely united to the object *is* absolute Being.

All things, and the whole universe of space and time, really exist and *are* in this third state; a state where every object (or portion of the whole) is united to every other object (or portion) by infinite threads of relation[1]—such infinitude of relations constituting the universal consciousness as embodied in that object. This

[1] Such a state is, of course, assumed by all physical science as the ground of its operations; and it is the (illusive) dream of science to be able to completely analyse it.

is the state of absolute Being in which all things *are*, and *from* which the things which we ordinarily see and know proceed by disintegration or ignorance. It is the state *from* which they lapse or fall by disintegration into ordinary consciousness or thought. That is to say, the real tree exists and can be seen in the resplendent light of the universal consciousness; but the tree which we ordinarily look upon is only the merest aspect of its infinitude, a few isolated thoughts or relations which the botanist or the woodman may happen to separate off and *call* the tree (the method of Ignorance).

All the universe exists, and is in this third state of consciousness; but we in the strange condition of illusion which belongs to the second stage—exiles from the Eden-garden, persuaded of the separateness of our individual selves, and unable to enter into true knowledge—are content to *gnaw* off tiny particles, which we call *thoughts*, from the great Reality. Assimilating and digesting these as best we can, we are persuaded that some day, putting all the results together, we shall arrive at the Reality. But the quest by this method is obviously hopeless. Infinities of infinity stretch before us, and vistas of brain-gnawing misery. Arrive doubtless we shall, but it will be by another route. One day when man has passed the 'rodent' stage he will enter quite naturally and normally into another world of being, surpassing that in which he now lives, as much as the present surpasses the world of simple consciousness belonging to the snail or the fish. Then, though he will perceive that his illusions of 'thought' and 'self' have not directly opened the door for him, he will find that they have fitted him for a realisation of the Truth, such as perhaps he could have obtained in no other way.

V

THE SELF AND ITS AFFILIATIONS

WE have seen three things in the two preceding papers—(1) that we first become conscious of the ego as part of the act of knowledge, and apparently inseparable from it; (2) that there is a stage of meagre false knowledge connected with the illusion of a separate self; and (3) a stage of full, vastly-extended knowledge connected with the (restored) sense of union between the ego and the object.

We have now to see how far we can get a clearer idea of what we mean by the ego or self.

But as a preliminary we may lay down two propositions, which will be useful later on. Firstly, though we are not conscious of the self except in some act of knowledge or consciousness of an object, and though consequently we cannot think of the self as existing altogether apart from knowledge, we *can* think of it as going to know, or having known (*i.e.* as potential of knowledge). Thus I think of myself as existing in sleep, as an ego that did know yesterday, or will know tomorrow, or I think of myself as perduring from one act of knowledge to the next, and so as it were forming a link between the two acts. This does not of course prove that I do so exist; and many psychologists argue that this idea is an illusion, and that the ego simply perishes in sleep, or with each act of knowledge—the reappearing ego in each case being an entirely new one. But practically we think as I have indicated; and in fact life being founded on this assumption (of the possibility of the duration of the ego in an unmanifested condition) we accept it—until such time as we find some explanation more adequate and satisfying.[1]

Secondly, this thought of the self as antecedently capable or potential of knowledge compels us to think of the knowledge as in some degree dependent on the self. In other words, since knowledge is always relative to the subject, the subject in every case contributes something without which the knowledge (at any rate in that form) would not exist. This flows obviously from things that have already been said, and it might seem unnecessary to dwell upon it; but it has important bearings.

Practically the matter is very evident. Not only awaking from sleep do we immediately recognise what the objects around us are, because, in fact, we have the memories or images of them already in our minds; but the simplest observation of things involves a similar antecedent condition—the *knowing what to look for.* How

[1] We shall see later that there is reason to believe that the ego in sleep passes into the third stage of consciousness.

hard to "find the cat" in the picture, or the wood-cock in the autumn leaves, till the precise image of what one wants to see is already in the mind, and then, how easy! The townsman walking along the high-road perceives not the hare that is quietly watching him from the farther field. Even when the countryman points it out with all circumstance, he fails; because the kind of thing he is to see is not already in his mind. Why is it so difficult to point the constellations to one who has never considered them before? The sky is simply a mass of stars, it is the *mind* that breaks it into forms. Or why, looking down from a cliff upon the sea, do we isolate a wave and call it *one?* It is not isolated; no mortal could tell where it begins or leaves off; it is just a part of the sea. It is not one; it is millions and millions of drops; and even these millions are from moment to moment changing, moving. Why do we isolate it and call it one? There is some *way of looking at things*, some preconception, already at work, in all cases, which determines or helps to determine, what we see, and how we see it. All nature thus is broken and sorted by the mind; and as far as we can see this is true of the simplest act of discrimination or sensation—the knower selects, supplies, ignores, compares, con tributes something without which the discrimination or sensation would not be.

Every one has experienced the magic of the musician, "that out of three sounds he frame, not a fourth sound, but a star." The three first notes are mere sounds, noises; but with the fourth, the phrase, the melody, the *meaning*, suddenly descends upon us from within; an answer comes from the background of our minds which transforms mere noise into music. Browning suggests that this magic is exceptional; but it is universal. All life is made of it. When the phrase or the melody have come to vibrate with meaning, then concatenations of phrases and melodies roll up into the huge symphony, which now we call an inspiration—though once it too was only noise. So too the incidents, the events, the meanings of life roll up. The trees, the mountains, people's forms and features, become luminous. Why do you see expressions, motives, emotions, in folk's faces, broad as day, which others never even suspect or imagine? The lines, the movements, are the same for everybody; but it is your mind that interprets. Always these knockings going on at the outer door of ourselves, and always something from within descending to answer—and ever new and newer answers as the years go on.

Nor does it seem by any means sufficient to explain these answers in each case as merely the result of summations or associations of previous experiences—partly because of the very *newness* of the answer (as of the 'star' in the music, or the expression on a loved one's face—things which though they may be called forth by experience are *like* no other experience); and partly because, as I have hinted, when we go back to the most primitive sensations we seem to find the same thing. Buried in the Self from the beginning are these affections. Browning indeed does not mention that exactly as the melody though made of or provoked by four sounds was utterly different from the four sounds or their summation, so each musical sound itself was a 'star' in comparison to the air-pulses that provoked *it*. Why should 270 taps in a second on the drum of the ear call forth the fairy C♯ from the hidden chambers within? or so many billions on the retina the magical and beautiful colour of *blue?* We cannot resist the conclusion that the *qualities* of things, the bitter, the sweet, the rough, the smooth, the lovable, the hateful, the musical, the brilliant are given already in the mind, though elicited by the outward phenomena, whatever they are; and that, allowing all we may for the gradual building up of knowledge from outside and its gradual transformation, there remain nevertheless the forms under which we receive this knowledge—from the mere sensations of touch or taste or colour or sound, up through the moral and mental qualities, to such things as the sense of self or of duty, and far beyond—which in a vast and ascending scale the ego, or hidden knower, contributes as its share to the solution of the marvellous problem!

Having then cleared the ground somewhat by means of these two preliminary propositions—(1) that the self or ego may (provisionally) be thought of as existent in sleep or in an unmanifested condition; and (2) that it must be thought of as contributing the (or a) formative element in the knowledge which comes to it—we may proceed farther on the way.

And first let us take, with respect to the nature of the self, the evidence of the third stage of Consciousness, such as we have it. We saw that in this third stage the subject and object are seen, are known, to be united, to be essentially one. This is the unanimous declaration of the witnesses, and we know also that the witnesses are by no means few or insignificant in the history of the world. If then we accept their evidence we must believe the final and real Self to be *one and universal.* For if A knows his essential identity with all the objects *a*, *b*, *c*, &c.; and B also knows the same; then A and B know their essential identity with each other, even though they may never have seen each other. And so on. All our 'selves' consequently must be one, or at least united so as to be branches of the One—even though for a time deluded by the idea of separation. The ground of the universe must be one universal Self or one Eternal City of selves, ever united and ever arriving at the knowledge of their union with each other.

But since the evidence of the so-called Cosmic Consciousness is yet scattered and unauthoritative, and by no means universally accepted, we may, in the second place, consider what proof we may be able to get from the ordinary processes of thought and consciousness. And even by these we seem to be led *towards* the same conclusion, and to have the way up the higher slopes indicated—though of course the mule stops short at the edge!

In fact, analysing one's own mind, one of the first things that appears is that the ego underlies or accompanies *every* thought. It is always I know, I think, I feel, I remember, I desire, I act. Though some thoughts are moderately simple, and some exceedingly complex, though some take their colour from others or derive a halo from the 'fringe' of unobserved thoughts round them,[1] still inevitably whether in the wholes or whether in the components the ego is there; and we become convinced at last that if we could reach even the simplest and most elementary sensation of which we are capable, the ego would underlie—would be a part of the knowledge, even though not distinctly differentiated in consciousness.

The ego, therefore, underlying my every possible thought—and even if I lived a thousand years and shared the thoughts of all folk on the globe, it would still underlie them—and underlying too the most elementary sensation I can

[1] By some it is supposed that it is by the action of this 'fringe' that the fourth note becomes a 'star'—by, in fact, waking myriads of unobserved associations. But again—though there is some truth in this view—we must note that the mere summation of associations, however numerous, will not create a new *feeling*. And we may also point out that the 'fringe' taken in an extended sense brings us back again to the unconscious, unmanifested ego.

possibly conceive myself having—cannot be a thought itself[1] And so we are forced to think of the ego either as a kind of unitary being *separate* from all thought (which of course won't do); or else as an infinitely complex unity capable of every conceivable thought—in fact a universal Being. But here, alas! we come to a fatal crevasse beyond which the four-footed creature cannot go. For as soon as we think *of* the ego, the ego has already become a thought and ceases to *be* the ego we are in search of. Obviously, therefore, thought can be no more made use of in the matter, and the only course that remains seems to be to *feel* (as we instinctively do) that the ego is a unitary Being; and to see that directly we try to *think* it, its first form is that of an infinite complex capable of every conceivable thought—

[1] Professor W. James suggests in speaking of the "stream of consciousness" that "the thoughts themselves are the thinkers!" ("Textbook of Psychology," p. 216.) But we really cannot accept this conundrum. I am *not* the knife which I handle or the ideal which I imagine. Practically the mind is compelled to believe in a self distinguishable from its own thoughts, something underlying and unitary which gives the sense and measure of sameness and continuity; and whatever subtleties may lead it away, the human mind will inevitably return to this view—the old antithesis of Being and Existence, of 'substance' and 'accident,' which cannot be avoided if we are to think at all. See also W. Wundt's "Human and Animal Psychology" (Sonnenschein, 1894), p. 250, where we read, "Self is not an idea—it is simply the *perception* of intercommunication of internal experience, which accompanies that experience itself." That is, the Self *is* the perception; the thoughts are the thinkers. But it is evident that this view creates more confusion than it dispels.

at the same moment acknowledging that in the act of thinking it we have already departed from its essence.

I shall now therefore assume, both on account of the direct evidence of the Cosmic Consciousness, and because the indirect evidence of the ordinary thought and consciousness points in the same direction, that there is a *real universal self*—a one absolute Ego and knower, underlying all existences—the *Tat tvam asi* of the Upanishads, the essence and life of the whole universe, and true self of every creature. And I think we are justified in assuming this, because clearly the evidence of the ordinary consciousness, however long we work at the problem, can never carry us a step farther than it does now; while on the other hand the direct evidence of the Cosmic Consciousness is added to by fresh witnesses every day, and daily becomes more conclusive.

There is therefore, I say, a real universal Self, but there is also an elusive self. There are millions of selves which are or think themselves separate. And over these we must delay. For to see the connection between them and the one Self is greatly important; and we may be sure that the illusive self is not for nothing; indeed the term 'illusive' may not after all be quite the right one to apply to it.

Let us ask two questions:—

1. How can the great Self also be millions of selves?

2. If the great Self is within each of us, and

the ego of every thought, why do we not know it so?

(1) How can the great Self also be millions of selves? Well, we may ask, How can the self of the human body also be millions of selves in the component cells of the body? For modern science more and more attributes selfness and intelligence to cells,[1] and more and more tends to establish the intimate relation between the self of the body and the selves of the cells. How can a man be one self in his office, and another at his club, and another in his domestic circle? How is it that plants and low animals multiply by fission? Do the selves multiply? Or, since a self is not necessarily to be thought of in space and time, can one self have many expressions in space and time, *i.e.* many bodies? or is it possible even that one self may *require* many bodies? Such are a few out of many questions that arise on the subject.

The fact remains apparently (though we are not in a position yet to see all round it) that a self *may* become many selves, or that it may have

[1] See Binet on the "Psychic Life of Micro-Organisms," where he maintains that infusoria exhibit memory, volition, surprise, fear, and the germinal properties of human intelligence. (Though such words as memory, volition, surprise, and fear must certainly be used with the greatest caution in this connection, yet the facts seem to show that there *is* a "sensibility" in these little creatures corresponding to the germ of these human faculties; and none the less real because it relates itself to chemical affinities. See H. S. Jennings on "The Psychology of a Protozoan," *American Journal of Psychology*, vol. x.)

many selves affiliated to it. In the human body the cells are differentiated in a vast number of ways, according to their service and function in the body. The intelligence of each cell is an aspect or a differentiation of the intelligence of the body. The great Self of the universe may differentiate itself into countless selves or 'aspects'—and this may be a condition of more perfect self-knowledge—yet each self or aspect may still be the whole and commensurate with the whole. "One eyesight does not countervail another," says Whitman. Ten thousand people gathered round an arena may see one another and the whole show, *each from his own point of view.* Each onlooker sums up the Whole, represents the Whole; but each from a different side. Each eyesight is individual and complete; yet it does not interfere with any other.

The fact is conceivable that the Self may become countless selves. The great Self is omnipresent in Space and Time; but if it appear or express itself at any one point of space and time (say as the ego of a single cell), then at once and in that moment it has determined an aspect of itself; and the ego in that cell is already an individual having within itself the potentiality of the whole, yet different[1] from every other possible individual of the universe. The fact of such multiplex appearance in Space

[1] Theoretically this would appear so—though the extreme conclusion (that every cell represents a separate and eternal Individuality) need hardly be pressed. (See next chapter.)

and Time is conceivable; the reason for it may be that of self-knowledge; but the "how" of the operation must necessarily remain inscrutable to our ordinary thought.

Leaving the matter thus, we may now then pass to the further question, (2) If the great Self is in each of us, and is the ego of every thought, why do we not know it so? And the answer is not difficult to frame. It is a question of *degree* of expression. We only know that of which we perceive the reflection.

Suppose the great Self, now incarnate as the ego of a single cell, to receive some simple sensation, to exercise some most primitive and elementary act of knowledge. Then, from what has been said a few pages back, it cannot do that except because the knowledge is in some sense implicit in itself, and *called forth* by the outer phenomenon (whatever that may be). There is a meeting of subject and object, a *reflection* of one in the other, a *consciousness*—but of very low degree. In the ego *all* knowledge (so we are at liberty to suppose) is implicit—yes, in the ego of that single cell—universal knowledge, as from that particular individual point of view. But that knowledge though implicit is not expressed; only the lowest degree of it has come into consciousness. The ego, therefore, has only to that degree become conscious of itself. Perhaps the sense of *touch* has wakened within it, but no more. Certainly the consciousness of its own universal being, of its true self, has not been excited or called forth.

As much of itself as has been reflected in the phenomenal world, it is conscious of with the order of consciousness that belongs to the phenomenal world, but no more.[1]

But presently another sensation comes along, or rather another happening which calls forth a sensation, say again of *touch*. Many such touches may come, and still there is no particular growth of consciousness. But one day the sense of *likeness* between them arrives. And it arrives from *within*. Doubtless there may be a real outer relation of likeness between the touches, or the objects that cause them; but until the ego sees and seizes that relation, contributes it from within itself, there is no sense or perception of likeness for it. Thus now the ego of that cell has arrived at the degree of consciousness represented by the sensation or perception ('recept') of likeness—

[1] Though our *thought* of course cannot compass this whole matter, we may help it out by the analogy of a fourth dimension. If this being which descends and manifests itself in tridimensional space is in fact a being of four-dimensional order, then that conception helps us to understand both its 'thereness' prior to manifestation, and the possibility of its manifestation being multiplex, though itself one. For if we suppose a three-dimensional object—say the hand with fingers downward—coming down into two-dimensional space—say the surface of still water, then we have a similar case. The hand is one, and it is 'there' prior to touching the water. Its first (multiplex) appearance on the surface is in four separate points, the finger-tips. Let us suppose now the *under* surface of the water to be a mirror, and suppose too the finger-tips to be provided with eyes; then as the fingers descend below the surface they will see themselves by reflection—first as mere nails, then as first joints, and so on; but always as entirely *separate* objects, till the moment when the body of the hand passing below the surface, reveals their union.

and it has arrived there by the way of reflection in the objective world.

It is clear that that ego being already a more or less individualised aspect of the universal Self, will see and seize and group the happenings of the external world in some degree differently from any other individual[1]—that is, its sensations and perceptions and inner qualities will develop and become manifest in consciousness according to its own law and order of exfoliation. The happenings of the external world will have their say certainly, and must not be minimised. They may retard or hasten the process; they may modify the outer embodiment; but it hardly appears that they can alter the general order of inner evolution.

As experiences multiply for our imagined ego at last a cluster of sensations, perceptions, latent associations, instincts, memories, thoughts, and feelings—fears, desires, wonderments—is formed about it, and float around. These are all qualities of the ego—active as well as passive—called forth doubtless by the outer world, and used to give form and outline to its dealings with the outer world, but coming down from within. They are exfoliations or expressions of the ego;[2]

[1] Though the differences, at any rate in the early stages, may be very slight.

[2] Thus the instinct of self-preservation and that of race-propagation appear in the very earliest creatures, long before actual self-consciousness has arisen—because, in fact, these instincts embody the primary need of the ego, *i.e.* that of expression — race-propagation being a device for securing expression in another organism when the first has perished.

they are the ego *coming* to consciousness of itself—but within every one of them lurks still the fathomless Being, and that which is unexpressed. This is the stage of Animal Consciousness, full of keen perceptions, sensations, instincts, and disclosing even higher powers of the mind; but still the thought of Self is not there; it has not yet come to reflection, to consciousness; the cluster of thoughts around the ego has not yet been distinctly conceived as a separate cluster—separate from the rest of the world; there is no knowledge of the real self, none of the illusive self even. Yet the thought of self must arrive some time, to give a further unity to all experience. It must arrive, and from within, because the self is a reality—in a sense the only reality[1]—and selfness must necessarily be one of the forms of its expression. But the mark of the individual Self is its differentiation, its distinctness, even in some degree its *separation* from the others. And so we find the first form in which the self fairly comes to consciousness is that of separation.

One day (and this happens probably in the higher animals, certainly in the human child) the thought of 'Me' arises; and from that moment a great new stage of evolution, of exfoliation, has begun—the stage especially of Humanity.

Now what is this thought of Me? It is evidently another generalisation, another form, which the ego at a certain stage projects, and

[1] Even as an individual the self is a reality through its affiliation to the great whole. It is a "son of God."

classifies and colours the world therewith. Just as at one stage in human evolution the sense of *melody* came with the power of giving new meaning to an otherwise disconnected series of sounds, so at another stage the sense of me-ness comes and throws a colour and an associative bond over all the experiences of the ego. "It is me," "It is mine." All this manifold cluster of thoughts and feelings is now grouped and conceived of as Myself, as Me.

And this is all right in a sense; for they are the expression (so far) of the great individual Ego. But it is clear that here two mistakes are inevitable to occur. In the first place, the little cluster is almost certain to be mistaken for a kind of fixed and final Me. It is looked upon as the real self, whereas at best it only represents the tiniest portion of the real self: it is, by the very act of being conceived, only an objectivation of the reality; while the ego itself sinks fathomless behind. And in the second place it (the Me) does not only appear as a complex of thoughts and feelings (representative of the ego), but is inevitably confused with the *objects* which excite those thoughts and feelings, which are the occasion of them, and in which they are reflected. Thus the body, the clothes, the goods, the possessions, are at first conceived as the Me. "They are me," "they are mine." It is as a child who, first seeing his reflection in a glass, thinks the reflection is the real thing, and something inherent in the glass, and in that special bit of glass. So the vast immortal Ego finds itself reflected, and first becomes conscious of itself (on this plane) as the local and limited Me, tangled apparently and bound in what are called material things.

From all this arise two illusions, inevitable to this stage of self-consciousness, and full of sorrow and suffering to mankind. The 'I' is thought of as perishable; and it is thought of as separate. It is thought of as separate, because the Me and the Mine (that is, the conditions and surroundings which reflect the I) are in these early stages quite local and limited, and therefore as long as the I is confused with the Me the self *must* be thought of not only as different, but as isolated, separate, enclosed, and apart from others.[1] And it is thought of as perishable, because it is confused with the things of the outer world and the perishing flux of phenomena.

But because, sitting on the bank of a stream, my reflection in the water wavers and shifts, that does not show that I am moving. Through a glass darkly we come at first to the knowledge of ourselves. For ages and ages the primitive Man peered in ponds and streams, in bits of shining flint or metal or shell, and saw strange obscure visions, which he credited to these objects, nor knew or perceived that they were dim images of his own person. Or if he did guess that they were images, he thought that he himself by some

[1] Hence, too, of course, the mind in this stage only functions in the second degree of consciousness, already described, in which subject and object are conceived of as separate.

magic was tangled in them.[1] Only at last, and with greater experience, did it one day flash upon him that He was different, and by no means to be confused with streams and shells. Only at last did his true identity come to him.

And only after long experience does the sense of our true Identity come to us. And as the civilised man who has learned what reflection is can now see his own face almost where he will —in pools and rivers and polished surfaces—nor thinks it only confined to some mystic shell or other object, so our true Identity once having been learned, our relation to our body having been completed, we shall find that the magic of one particular body is no longer necessary, since out of the great ocean of Nature we can now pick up our own reflection (or make to ourselves a body of some kind) practically anywhere.

So for a long time the 'Me' goes on growing. Every new thought or experience that is added sinks into the Me; and as long as the ruling idea —of the Me as a *separate perishable* entity— governs the cluster or organism, so long do greed and fear, hatred and jealousy, sorrow and grief, increase and multiply and hover round, till their presence grows wellnigh insupportable. Yet all the time the ego, the real self, is behind, waiting for its next development, its next expression— which must inevitably come.

[1] Hence the universal dread among primitive folk of having likenesses or images of themselves made, and their fear of the enchantment of mirrors.

We have dealt much in similes. Let us return once more to the child regarding its own reflection —say in the tiniest of tiny pools. So small is the little mirror that it only reflects the smallest part of the child—a lock of hair, a portion of its dress. The child does not in the least recognise what the reflection is. But it has a water-can and pours water into the pool, and the pool grows. Now the child can see its own entire hand in the water. It is fascinated, and tires not to pose its fingers in every way for reflection. But again the pool goes on growing, and more of its body becomes visible, till at last, lo! the child can see itself complete.

So to us. Each new thought, each new experience that is added to the Me, is like a drop of water that is added to the pool,[1] till it becomes large enough—the Me becomes sufficiently universal—to reflect the universality of the I. The vision of the true Self at last arises, with wonder and revelation and joy indescribable: the vision of a self that is united to others, that is eternal. The thoughts connected with separation and mortality—the greeds, the fears, the hatreds, the griefs fall off—and a new world, or conception of the world, opens—life is animated with a new spirit. The Me-conception (as far as that means isolation, mortality, 'self-seeking') disappears, is broken up, is transformed; and the life is transformed accordingly.[2]

[1] Added really in the last resort by ourselves.

[2] Always the life, the vitality, of an organism is a reflection of its overmastering thought or conception, and in the main is determined thereby.

When I say the idea of the true Self arises, I do not say that at once the complete and final Individual is realised. Nature does not proceed *per saltum*. On the side of the past, there may yet be much "clinging to the old self"; and again, on the side of the future, there may be many new disclosures and revelations still to be made. But this stage—in which the human being *begins* at least to realise his universal life and identity; in which he, as it were, comes within sight of the end—forms such an epoch, that it may be taken as one of the great landmarks on his immense journey—a landmark more important even than that which signalled the birth of Self-consciousness.

It marks the entrance to an emancipated, glorified, transformed Humanity, of whose further course and transformation we need not too curiously inquire, though we seem to discern dimly its grander lines.[1] It marks the arrival of the third stage of Consciousness, at first only occasionally and spasmodically realised, but even so guiding and pointing the way; and finally becoming permanent—not necessarily to obliterate and negate the earlier faculties, but rather to interpret and render them for the first time really rational and meaningful. It marks the realisation at last of the whole meaning of the Universe, even though the detail thereof may be for ever inexhaustible.

With a kind of inexorable logic, from infinitely various beginnings, from infinitely various sides,

[1] See chap. xiii., "Transformation."

the Great Self sums itself up to form a vast affiliation of selves—a Celestial City of equals and lovers.[1] "It is by love only that we can fully enter into that harmony with others which alone constitutes our own reality and the reality of the universe. We conceive the universe as a spiritual whole, made up of individuals, who have no existence except as manifestations of the whole; as the whole, on the other hand, has no existence except as manifested in them."[2]

[1] Love, as we have already indicated, whether taken in its most ideal or its most sensuous signification, is a form of the Cosmic Consciousness.

[2] M'Taggart, "The Further Determination of the Absolute," p. 56.

VI

THE SELF AND ITS AFFILIATIONS

(Continued)

HAVING in the last paper considered the Self and its affiliations from the within point of view, we may now with advantage study the same subject on its more external side.

A certain school of psychologists, in trying to explain the total consciousness of an organism as the sum (in some sense) of the consciousnesses of its separate cells, are met with serious criticism, and themselves find a difficulty, in the question of how the separate cell-consciousnesses can possibly be fused in one consciousness, or how even we can conceive such a thing. How can one cell know, it is said, what its neighbour feels, or fuse its neighbour's experience with its own? What kind of total ego is it that can possibly gather up the experiences of millions of lesser egos, and render them one? And the difficulty is perfectly natural, and indeed insuperable, as long as the egos of the cells are held to be distinct and separate. But as soon as we see that (as suggested in the last chapter) they may be the *same*, that they may be already one, the difficulty disappears. We have, indeed, arrived at the conclusion that all egos *are* finally the same, though differing little or much in aspect, in affiliation, in ramification—even as every twig on a tree dates back to the trunk, and has a common life with the others, however different from them in aspect to the outer world, or in affiliation to its main stem, it may be. And so it is not difficult to conceive of them as fusing their knowledge. Indeed it is inevitable that they should do so.

Let us consider for a moment the genesis of the body, human or other. The body grows from one cell, sperm and germ united. The cell obtains nourishment (from the organism of the mother, in the higher creatures), and grows, and splits into two, four, many, and then multitudes of cells, which dispose themselves into certain forms—the outlines of the growing creature. At the same time, the dividing and multiplying cells become differentiated from each other, and finally (in the human being) break up into some thirty well-marked varieties, according to their uses and functions in the complete organism.

[To make the meaning of this process clear, we must remember that we were compelled to think of the ego of that primitive cell as itself a unitary but enormously complex being, *manifested* at first in the lowest degree. Then we see the multiplication and differentiation of that cell simply as the process by which the various complexities of its inner Being are further manifested

—their manifestations, no doubt, being sundered in the world of space, but their inner nature losing nothing of its original unity.]

To proceed. The growing, multiplying, differentiating cells are all in touch and in relation with each other; but in time by special nerve-channels (themselves composed of cells) more special and closer relations are established, groups are formed, which tend to act and to feel together; and again in time some of these groups unite and form larger groups, and so on up to the whole organism. As to the nerve-channels, which represent at any rate the subtler and swifter and more specialised relations (though not by any means *all* the relations), they are of various kinds and structure, and are minutely distributed over the whole body; and the nerve-centres and plexuses, which bring these relations to definite focus in a vast variety of ways, are also widely distributed, not only in the brain and encephalon, but all down the spinal cord, and in the trunk of the body, where they lie embedded among the organs.

Such is the process of the growth of the body; and such—as we have seen—or very similar, is the growth of the mind. In fact in the case of the latter (using the word 'thought' to cover all affections of the mind) we have seen that a very primitive or elementary thought must first appear, that this being fed and added to by the happenings of the outer world, repeats itself and multiplies, and becomes differentiated into other nearly-resembling thoughts, and that by degrees the ego groups these elementary thoughts into more inclusive thoughts (as when it groups a number of separate pulses into a musical sound), and then these group-thoughts again into higher group-thoughts (as when it groups musical sounds into melodies or harmonies). And as in this mental process we are compelled to think of the same ego which underlies the total mind, or one of the higher group-thoughts, as underlying also the more elementary thoughts (the same 'I' that perceives the melody perceiving also the separate notes); so we may seem justified in supposing in the case of the bodily cells that their myriad egos form what may be called a group-soul—that they are in fact one and the same with the soul of the whole body.

The difference is, of course, that in the simple cell, though the total ego is 'there,' it is necessarily expressed only to a very simple and primitive degree, whereas in the groups of cells, especially when the latter have reached some degree of differentiation, it may be much more fully expressed. We can hardly refuse too to think that not only complexity but *volume* of feeling depends to some extent on the largeness of the group of cells concerned. Thus in the great emotions—fear, anger, &c.—it is obvious that vast multitudes of cells are agitated, whole organs affected, secretions changed, and so forth. But in pure thought or representation where no emotion is concerned (as, for instance, in simply using the word 'fear') there is no sense of volume, and probably quite a few little cells in the brain, specially differentiated to express that simple concept, are all that is required. There is no feeling probably which carries with it more permanent volume, as well as a great degree of complexity, than that of selfness; and we may associate that with the supposition that roughly speaking *all* the cells of the body (through their instinct of self preservation, if through nothing more complex) are concerned in it.

I think myself (subject of course to correction) that it is a mistake to suppose that consciousness is limited to the cells in a certain portion of the brain. The hypothesis does at its best sound very improbable. Certainly it is likely that the cells of the cortex are specialised in that direction (and particularly as representatives of the *second* stage of consciousness); but this would not imply that other cells—from which the cerebral cells have been differentiated — have not the same faculty in less degree. To even the simplest tissue-cell one must credit sensibility, to the nerve-cells higher sensibility; to others perhaps, as those of the Sympathetic system, simple consciousness; to the brain-cells or groups self-consciousness; and there must be many cells or groups which represent those higher orders of consciousness of which we are occasionally aware.

That there *is* a diffused consciousness all through the body, I think any one who attends to the subject will feel persuaded—and that, in some sense, independent of the brain.[1] It is, in fact, the primitive consciousness out of which the more complex brain-consciousness has been evolved; and it links on to that 'subliminal' region of the mind of which we have heard so much lately—the vast 'fringe' of thought and feeling which surrounds our ordinary consciousness, which never comes quite into the full light of observation, and yet is always obscurely present.

In these lights it does not seem difficult to think of the egos of the body-cells as one with the total Ego which represents the fusion of their separate consciousnesses—one with it, though each less adequately manifested than the whole. And indeed I believe they love to feel this affiliation; dimly they are conscious of it, and it vitalises them, presiding over and directing their activities.

Now here we have to pause; for indeed if my conscious Ego and the egos of all my body-cells

[1] Stanley in his "Evolutionary Psychology of Feeling" (p. 32) says: "In man, physiologically speaking, it is the brain-consciousness that is general. But we need not suppose this to extinguish all the lower ganglionic consciousness from which it arose." And Ribot in his "Psychology of the Emotions" (p. 200), speaking of the nutritive functions, says: "Though in the adult they play only a latent and intermittent part [in consciousness] by reason of the preponderance of external sensations, images, and ideas, yet it is probable that in animals, particularly in voracious ones, the functions are inverted, and that cœnæsthesia passes to the front rank." In fact since the brain-cells are only differentiations of the primitive body-cells, we are compelled to think of the general cells as having a germinal consciousness; and though they may convey their cœnæsthesia or common sentiment to the brain, it no less originates, and has its first birth in them.

were in the condition of harmony suggested, all would be "pancakes and cream": the state of affairs indicated in the former chapter, "The Art of Creation," would be realised; these bodies of ours, and the bodies of other creatures, trees, plants, &c., would be the adequate manifestations (so far) of their respective egos, and would be the forms under which we should apprehend the expression of our own and other minds.

Yet clearly this is not so. I and my cells fall out to some extent. They do not always do or say what I want. There are *con*fusions as well as fusions, alterations and alternations of personality. My body is *not* altogether an embodiment of my mind—at any rate of that mind of which I am preponderantly conscious.

What is the cause of this discrepancy—or of these discrepancies?

This leads us on to further considerations.

Exactly as a (human) body is a complex of cells descended and differentiated from a single pair, so is a (human) Race a complex of bodies, which for our present purpose we may suppose as descended and differentiated from a single pair. I am not alluding to Adam and Eve especially as progenitors of the whole human race, but rather (in order to gain clearness) to smaller tribes and peoples—such as the Maoris, or the Apache Indians, or the old Israelites—much interrelated, and in many cases descended from a very few progenitors, if not actually (as their traditions often relate) a single pair. Such a race has all the characteristics of an organic being: it has its well-marked customs, instincts, religion, ideals, external habits of life, grade of mental development, and so forth. It has its individual members, its groups, and larger groups, culminating in the whole tribe or race as an entity, just the same as the cells with regard to the human body. And it has its phases of emotion and belief and action—its patriotisms, religions, and warlike and other enthusiasms—belonging to it only *as* a whole, and called forth somehow by the sentiment of the whole. "Crowds are sometimes accessible to a very lofty morality," says a French writer[1]—"a much loftier one, indeed, than that of which the isolated individual is capable." And anyhow we see that societies, not only of bees (as Maeterlinck has shown), but of all creatures, up to man, have, *quâ* societies, a life of their own inclusive of and superadded to that of their individual members.

It is difficult therefore, in view of all this, to refuse to credit an Ego and a consciousness to a well-marked race or people or tribe; and of course this has often been done; while the cognate idea of the "social organism" has become a thing of common acceptance. Now if this ascription of an organic and conscious life to huge collections of human beings were merely an abstract affair, like Auguste Comte's "Humanity" or the Spencerian "social organism," it would be, to say the least, a trifle dull and uninteresting. But the

[1] G. Le Bon, "Psychologie des foules," p. 46.

moment we realise that it means just the opposite—something very much alive indeed, and entangled in the very heart of our own natures—then it becomes absorbingly important. Not only do we recognise, when these huge crowd-emotions come along, that immense unsuspected forces are working within us; but we see that at all times, in some mysterious way, the capacity of entering into the Race-consciousness is in us, and that daily and hourly this fact is moulding and modifying our lives: just the same as in every limb of my body there lurks the capacity of being thrilled by the great emotions of my total ego, and this fact in its turn guides and moulds the destinies and activities of my tiniest cells.

To the more detailed consideration of this subject, and of the way in which the gods, the devils, and the great emotions represent our past in the Race-consciousness, I have given the next four chapters, so I will not dwell upon it here. We may here consider more in detail the mode of arrival of the individual ego on the scene, and his relation to the race-life.

How did I arrive as regards the race to which I belong? Why, the *same protozoic cells* (same in fundamental nature, or *ego*, and same by sheer continuity of life) which were in Adam and Eve have also produced me.[1] Or, to bring the matter

[1] The *immortality* of the protozoic cells is now widely accepted. That is to say, since these cells multiply by fission or gemmation, they do not die. If a parent cell divides into two (or four) descendant cells, the descendant cells are simply a prolongation and multiplication of the parent life, and continuous

within more definite compass, the same cells from which Abraham and his wife Sarah sprung, produced also Solomon and St. Paul. [I select the Jews as an illustration, because they afford an instance of a very well-defined race which, notwithstanding occasional lapses, kept itself very pure and unmixed, and, as a consequence, had the strictest customs and religious ideals, and the strongest national consciousness.] That is to say, to put the matter more definitely still, the sex-cells of Abraham and Sarah united to form a single cell, from which Isaac sprang. Every cell in Isaac's body was therefore a prolongation and fission-growth from that single cell. Isaac in his turn uniting with Rebekah (his cousin) similarly produced Jacob, who again uniting with Leah (his cousin), produced Reuben, Simeon, and Judah; and so on. After endless ramifications in this tree

with it, and so on to any number or degree of descendants. Any one of these descendant cells of course may perish by accident, but the point is that the descendant or descendants in the hundredth generation still will be the *same*, in being and life, with the parent cell. That it or they will have learned much on the way can hardly be doubted. Whether they will have been modified by the outer world is a point which, with regard to the sex-cells, Weismann has challenged. That the sex-cells learn, by long practice, skill in the art of self-expression is obvious from the facts of embryology and "recapitulation"; and this in itself is a kind of use-inheritance. Herbert Spencer in his "Facts and Fragments" has given reasons for supposing that even with the acceptance of Weismann's general views, use-inheritance is quite possible; and the most reasonable theory of the whole subject seems to be that a great inner law of growth presides in the evolution of races and species, but always subject to a slow modification by the outer world in the forms of Use-inheritance and Natural Selection.

of life, Solomon appeared, and again after more, St. Paul or Jesus. The conclusion is clear. Remembering the immortality of the cells and their continuity of life, with of course great differentiations and ramifications all down the centuries, we see that a tiny group of cells in Abraham's time, themselves related to each other, and probably differentiations of some one cell further back, lay beneath the whole development of the Jewish race through the centuries; and that this latter indeed might reasonably be looked upon as the exfoliation of a single Ego which through this long chain, in hundreds of thousands of lives affiliated to it, *sought* expression, and so far succeeded in finding it.

Well might Jesus of Nazareth exclaim, "Before Abraham was, I am." His consciousness, the consciousness of his own being, had reached that depth at which it had become united with the consciousness of the race; and in using those words he merely stated a fact which he felt within himself, and knew to be true.

In this view we see and understand the enormous import and sacredness of sex, and its deep association with the religious and communal life of the race—a thing which the earlier and less mixed races understood instinctively and appreciated much better than we do, but which (for reasons which may later appear) has been to a great degree lost in the modern societies and nations. The sex-cells, conserved and perpetuated by each organism, and passed on with fervent care from generation to generation, are the most central and potent, and least differentiated of all the cells of the body—the other cells losing their reproductiveness in proportion as they are more and more differentiated. They are the most representative of the body and all its faculties, and within them lies the secret and heart of the race.[1]

The same ever-descendant cells, I say, which produce the first man of a race, produce the last man. But the last man is not therefore the same as the first man. The first man may be merely a living soul (or psyche), the last may be a quickening Spirit. The little primitive cell may grow and differentiate and grow, till that which was in it attains at last to Manhood and Deliverance. The descendant cells by ever-renewed practice, generation after generation, in the expression of the Ego within them, may attain more and more facility; the art of building up the body, tentative at first, by repetition becomes easy; and if the potency of the cells continues (which without a crossing of the strain with another race, or branch of the great Ego, does not always take

[1] Ray Lankester (quoted by Geddes and Thomson, "Evolution of Sex," p. 277) says, "The bodies of the higher animals which die, may from this point of view be regarded as something temporary and non-essential, destined merely to carry for a time, to nurse, and to nourish the more important and deathless fission-products of the unicellular egg." And Metchnikoff ("The Nature of Man," p. 268) remarks: "Scientific proof exists therefore that our bodies contain immortal elements, eggs, or spermatozoa. . . . These cells not only are truly alive, but exhibit properties that are within the category of psychical phenomena." He also says, "It is possible to speak of the soul of protozoa."

place) the race in question may reach a high level of development.

Thus when a man to-day, born of such and such parents, appears, his body in its early stages is rapidly and instinctively built up; these stages summing up and embodying the evolution of the race behind it. His ego is already affiliated to that of the race; and his unfoldment (so far) already prepared. His body, so far, represents a summation of an endless series of mental actions preceding his actual nativity, a ramifying thread of race-life, here condensed. All the instincts, all the devices, all the mental and physical adjustments by which during the centuries the Ego obtained expression for its own nature and qualities *amid the outer conditions in which the race existed*, are (together with that nature and those qualities) summed up and represented in his corporal organism; and within it the immense heritage of race-memory is stored. The 'I,' the Ego, of his race is not only present, manifesting itself in Time and History—but an aspect, an affiliation, of it is now, to-day, present and existent in that man, in his Body.

And this brings us back to that discord or discrepancy between the body and the conscious self, which started the subject of the last few pages. Is there reason for supposing a real discord between the Ego of the race, and the self-conscious individual who is affiliated to it? and is there in the body of the individual man really in some sense a seat of race-consciousness, separate from his brain, or that part of it, which is the seat of his ordinary mind?

To take the last question first. We have already suggested that there is a consciousness belonging peculiarly to the body and its 'automatic' nerve-centres and ganglia, with all their instincts, habits, and organic functioning. Though these (partly from our inattention to them) appear as a rule dark and silent, and beyond the region of our voluntary observation or control, yet it is becoming more and more admitted that there is a sort of 'awareness' of them. Science is less and less able to proceed without the conception of the 'subliminal' mind, or the 'subjective,' or the 'subconscious,' or the 'fringe' which surrounds the ordinary consciousness; it is more and more seen that the emotions are forms of consciousness accompanying the organic functions and secretions, and that all the processes of the body contribute their flow great or small to the life of the feelings, which again expresses itself in the life of the intellect; there are facts such as second-sight, telepathy, and luminous sleep, which indicate states of consciousness existing when the ordinary brain is at rest; there are the facts of cosmic consciousness already alluded to; and lastly, there is a whole series of facts with which I shall deal in the next chapters, which seem to show that there is such a thing as a race-consciousness associated with our bodily organisation and accessible on occasions to our conscious minds.

I do not doubt that the body and its organisation are the scene and the seat of an extensive consciousness—of other orders of consciousness—which, though usually hidden from, or unrecognised by, us are still really operating within and around our minds, and are directly accessible to them.[1]

But whatever consciousness may have its seat in the body, or the cerebellum, or the automatic portions of the brain, and however vast the summation and expression of experience and instinct these may represent, they still do not represent the *total* possible expression of the Ego within. The body (at any rate in childhood) represents only the expression to which the race has attained so far. There are vast deeps of the unexpressed yet behind it. And a *progressive* power is needed to seek and search and devise and effect ever new advances of expression—however slight. This power is the conscious Brain. It is the function of the Brain to be continually making new combinations in which the whole *Feeling*-nature can find satisfactions—in other words, to be continually extending the area of expression of that nature. Ever new thoughts, ever new adjustments, ever new combinations, it consciously

[1] There is much to show that animals have some kind of direct consciousness of their internal functions; and the Hindu yogis, who have given much attention to this subject, not only obtain a marked consciousness of their own internal organs, but an extraordinary power of voluntarily controlling them—suspending at will the action of the heart, for instance, or reversing the peristaltic movements of the alimentary canal.

forms—which, as they are finally accepted and grow habitual, fall back into the so-called unconscious mind of the organism, and are replaced by new purposive endeavours.

The Conscious Mind (of the second stage) is the pioneer of progress. If we take it as represented by the Brain, and if we take the subconscious hereditary Mind to be in the main represented by the Great Sympathetic Nerve-system, then the discord or discrepancy to which we have alluded is that between the conscious and the subconscious Minds, between the Brain and the Great Sympathetic.[1] The discord *is* to a certain extent the progress; and therefore we need not look upon it as bad. It is easy to imagine, and common to observe, that a considerable and rapid mental advance may bring us into conflict with our hereditary thought and habits.[2] Nevertheless such conflict is uncomfortable and must not be allowed to continue long, at risk of mental or bodily disease. It may indicate either that the hereditary attitude has to be modified, or possibly on the other hand that a mental position has been rashly taken up which may have to be abandoned or altered. The Brain may be at fault, or, on the other hand, the Great Sympathetic may be. Diseases are not unfrequently

[1] More strictly speaking, between the fore-brain or Cerebrum on the one hand, and the Great Sympathetic *plus* the hind-brain and the spinal system on the other.

[2] Metchnikoff suggests that some "disharmonies" in Man are caused by his highly developed Brain bringing him into "a new path of evolution."

the clearing and expiation of this conflict, and in that sense they too are not always to be regretted, nor necessarily to be looked on as retrogressions. But this subject, which is a large one, cannot be fully considered here.

The Conscious Mind we may then regard as the latest outgrowth and expression of the unfolding Ego; and in that sense it is very important. But to expect our bodies at every moment to transform themselves into expressions of its passing moods would be an absurd thing to do. It is only the advance guard, as it were, of a moving column; the bud on the branch; the crest on the wave. And it is easy to see that *without* the other — without the subconscious Mind and the life of the Body, without the great race-Mind behind it (and those other orders of consciousness) to which it is affiliated, it is but a very poor thing, and of comparatively little scope and value.

It is perhaps the fault of the modern Brain or conscious Mind that it has not perceived this. From the moment when the sense of Self (as a separate being) evolved within primitive man, and entered into distinct consciousness, from that moment an immense stimulus was given to the Brain or the conscious Mind (to devise satisfactions and expressions for the individual self as apart from the race); and the enormous development of brain-power and thought (all in the second stage of consciousness) during the period of Civilisation goes with this fact. On which indeed we may congratulate ourselves; but it has led to a fearful, and for the time being most sinister, divorce between the two parts of man's nature. Amid the clatter of self-interests and self-conscious brain activities, the presence and the functioning of other orders of mind within us have been discounted and disregarded; and, cut off from the mass and communal life around him, from the race-life behind, and the heaven-life within, the little self-conscious man has become a puny creature indeed.

We must in the future look to a restoration of the harmony between (roughly speaking) the Mind and the Body, the Brain and the great Sympathetic, the conscious and the subconscious Man. "Why," asks Mr. W. H. Hudson in his last nature-story,[1] "why does the brightness of the mind [so often] dim that beautiful physical brightness which the wild animals have?" The *recovery* of the organic consciousness, the realisation of the *transparency* of the body and the splendour of its intuitions, is not an impossible feat. The Hindus and other Orientals have in these directions, partly by deliberate practice, come into touch with and command of regions whose existence the Western peoples hardly suspect. In the West, the modern upgrowth of Woman and her influence will ere long make possible a Humanity which shall harmonise even in each individual the masculine and the feminine elements, and bring back at last the Brain and the self-conscious mind into

[1] "Green Mansions."

relation with that immense storehouse of agelong knowledge and power which is represented by the physical body in the individual, as it is represented by the communal life and instinct in the mass-people.

Thus finally, looking back on what has been said, we see that the whole of Creation falls together into expressions of the One endless, boundless, fathomless Self and its myriad affiliations—expressions reached by infinite divisions into, and differentiations, fusions, and concatenations of the primitive elements of consciousness. Cells, plants, lichens, molluscs, fish, quadrupeds, bee and insect swarms, birds, planets, solar systems, races of men and animals, societies—organisms far-stretching in *time* as well as in space—all illustrate this conception. The whole of Creation is *alive*. But we now understand, when we look at a man or a bee, that we are not looking at a little separate being that has sprung as it were full-armed out of the ground in the course of a few days or years, and whose actions and perceptions are rounded by that scope; but that we are looking at a being who stretches (through affiliation after affiliation) into the far "backward and abysm of Time," who through endless centuries has been seeking to express itself; nevertheless whose consciousness is *here and now* in its visible body, as well as in that agelong world-life. The ego of the Bee, we understand, is not a perishable thing of six or seven weeks' duration, but is in its essence one with the "Spirit of the Hive" (whence comes the utter readiness of the Bee to give its little body for the safety of the Hive); the particular hive or colony of bees again is affiliated to the whole race of domestic bees, and this again to the further back race of wild bees; and when our little friend comes humming along the southern wall among the early blooms in the February morning she brings (as we feel) a message not of the moment, but of things æonian slumbering deep in our hearts as well as in hers.

This *aliveness* of all Nature, and its derivation from one absolute and eternal Self, must be realised. And if at times the multiplexity of egos, as of gnats in the summer sunshine, in myriad procession and endless turmoil, seems appalling and fatiguing; then at other times their fusion and affiliation with each other into larger and grander beings of comparative fewness seems consoling; and even the conclusion of their ultimate Oneness may bring a sense of immense majesty and calm—which, if it should be touched with melancholy, would lead us back quite naturally to the multiplexity again[1]

We may envisage the matter as we like, and according to our mood. Sufficient that it is a *fact*, which we have to realise: we may say, *the* fact of the universe.

Let us return for a moment to the elementary act of knowledge or perception, from which we started four chapters back. I come to the gate of a wood and see, before me, the massed foliage and congregated stems. It seems a little matter, but within that simple act sleep the immensities. I am an artist, and the light and shade and colour attract me, rousing emotions which I do not analyse; the whisper of the leaves and the songs of the birds wake far-back feelings dating from ancestral ages. I am a woodman, and I see the size and quality of the timber; all the adjuncts of wood-craft—the brushing, the peeling, the felling, and the hauling with horses—rustle around me; and dim visions rise of the log-cabins or wattled huts in which my forefathers lived. The mystery, in either case, and the wild life of the woods are there, though unseen; and the instincts which led the Britons to seek them for a cover and a refuge, or the Druids to hold their worship among them. All these things are present somehow in that act of perception. And so are the far remembrance of fear and primitive terror, the vision of nymphs and wood-gods, and things deep down in the life of the animals, and of the trees themselves, or even in the life of the planet. A wonderful aura and halo surrounds that little scene from the gate, and is latent in its every detail. The young moon sails above in the pure sky of evening, and an immense peace, as of some eternal being, descends, folding in silence the soul of the onlooker.

The knowledge of our unfathomable life is implicit in every least act of perception. Nor does it bar the expression of our most determined individuality. Nay, it needs this *for* its expression. It stands revealed and manifest in the words and actions of humanity's best-loved children.

"Afar down I see the huge first Nothing, I know I was even
there,
I waited unseen and always, and slept thro' the lethargic mist,
And took my time, and took no hurt from the fetid carbon.
Long I was hugg'd close—long and long.
Immense have been the preparations for me,
Faithful and friendly the arms that have help'd me.
Cycles ferried my cradle, rowing and rowing like cheerful boatmen,
For room to me stars kept aside in their own rings."

So says Whitman of the past—and we need not doubt his word. And again of the future:—

"It avails not, time nor place—distance avails not,
I am with you men and women of a generation, or ever so many
generations hence."

And again Jesus of Nazareth says:—

"Lo! I am with you alway, even unto the end of the world."

VII

PLATONIC IDEAS AND HEREDITY

THOUGH experience coming from the outer world affects the Mind (through the senses), yet the way this experience is seized and combined is largely given by the Mind itself. There is, as we have already said, a subjective element in all knowledge—and without it there can be no knowledge.

This subjective element may arise from previous experience, as when we recognise the hare sitting in its 'form' in a distant field because we have already seen other hares so sitting, perhaps much nearer. The mind is ready, as it were, to take the required shape and attitude, and may do so even under doubtful or misleading circumstances, because it has taken the same shape and attitude so often before. And we can hardly doubt that through heredity also, in some way, as well as through our own individual experience, the mind acquires the habit of making certain combinations and interpretations of the outer world.

But it is also obvious that there is a great deal on the subjective side of knowledge which is given antecedently to *all* experience, hereditary or individual—as when the sense of *likeness* or *difference* arises, or of *size*, or of *number*; or when so many taps on the ear combine to a musical *sound*, or so many vibrations in the optic nerve to the impression of *blue* or *red;* or when sounds combine to a sense of *harmony* or of *melody;* or when certain vibrations and agitations of the body coalesce to the emotion of *fear*, or other vibrations and agitations to *love;* or when certain perceptions grouped together give rise to the sense of *justice*, or of *truth*, or of *beauty*.

In all these cases, though the mental state thus produced may grow from small beginnings and by means of experience, yet it is in a sense prior to experience—that is to say, it is inconceivable that a succession of taps on the drum of the ear should be combined into one and heard as a single musical sound, unless the power of so combining taps was in the mind prior to experience. Or it is clear that two sounds might go on side by side in the ear for ever, and not be heard as harmony, unless the mind added to the two that third and separate thing which *is* the sense of their harmony. Certainly the sense of harmony might at first be felt in some very simple relation of two notes, and afterwards might grow and be extended to much more remote and multiplex relations; but all the same it would from the first be an original synthesis contributed from within. So of the sense of likeness or difference. In whatever undeveloped mind of infant or animal it first occurs to feel that two experiences, not only are each *what* they are, but that they are like or unlike each other, the new experience (of likeness or unlikeness) is something added by the mind. It represents a new power or faculty developed, and totally unlike all its former powers and faculties.

So again when a great number of inchoate movements in the tissues and nerves of the body, and agitations of the muscles, organs and secretions, with the internal sensations they convey, are all combined in one emotion of fear, or another set of movements and sensations in one emotion of love, these emotions are totally different from the sensations and movements so combined. They are something added by the mind to the group of sensations; they are its way of seizing and combining the group. Lastly, certain groups of experiences excite in our minds the sense of Justice or of Truth or of Beauty; but we are utterly unable to conceive that these great ideas are in the separate experiences or events themselves, but they are our way of looking at them, our *feeling* with regard to them.

I have insisted on the aspect of all these things as feelings. They are sensations, emotions, states or affections of the Mind. They are the *qualities* given by the mind to its various combinations of experience. Time, Space, and Causality, said Kant, are universal forms or qualities of the understanding—conditions of our perception of outer experience. But (we may say) redness, blueness, sound, heat, similarity, order, harmony, love, justice, beauty, &c., are *qualities* given by the mind still deeper down, and projected by it into the world of space, time, and causality. They are the names for feelings, states, or *ideas*, if we like to call them so, aboriginal and primitive in the mind itself.

And here comes in a most important point—the distinction, namely, between the two aspects of each of these things—the inner or the outer, the emotional or the intellectual, the synthetic or the analytic: the neglect of which distinction has been the cause of endless confusion.

In fact, we see that each of these affections (the experience of a musical sound, for example, or of similarity, or of justice) is on one side a perfectly simple and undecomposable feeling; while on the other side it resolves itself into a relation, possibly quite complex, between objects. Thus the sound of a violin string is on its inner and deeper side a simple and unique sensation, but in its more external and analytic aspect it appears as a series of vibrations of very complex form falling in a particular way on the ear. *Similarity* is from one point of view a simple state or affection of the mind, from the other it figures out in the form of multiplex relations between objects. So of Justice; on the one side all the labyrinthine detail of statutes and courts of law; on the other a severe unique sentiment. Herbert Spencer has a long and eloquent passage in which he shows analytically and from the intellectual side the vast complexity of *love*. Dr. Bucke says that love is a perfectly simple moral state defying analysis!

It is obvious that unless we recognise the

two-sidedness of these mental states, we are liable to be landed in the utmost confusion. Let us call such a mental state (following the nomenclature of Plato, but perhaps somewhat extending it), which on its inner side appears as a simple quality or feeling, but on its outer side is a structure more or less complex, an "idea." Then the units of the mind's operations are such ideas, which on one side are relations, and on the other side are simple structureless feelings.[1] But it is to be noted that the latter side seems to be the more intimate and essential, because the same feeling may be associated with more than one set of relations—as when the sense of harmony in music is provoked by more than one chord, or the sense of injustice by various possible relations between folk.

There is another point which must be noted, *i.e.* the structure of ideas with regard to one another. Thus, to take the case of music, to which we have so often referred: taps on the ear combine to the sensation or idea of sound; but the sensations of sound combine to the idea of harmony or of melody. Harmonies and melodies again combine to a much more complex structure—a musical phrase. This structure in its turn wakes an *emotion*, which is, as it were, the other side of it. Whenever we hear the phrase the same emotion

[1] The distinction between "ideas" and *concepts* must be clearly held in mind. The concept of a dog is a purely intellectual abstraction—a symbol, so to speak, of dogs in general—with no feeling necessarily attached to it. An idea is not an idea unless it carries with it feeling and power.

recurs. Finally, a whole series of phrases, with their accompanying emotions, make up a musical piece, which excites in us some still grander synthesis and sense of Beauty or Truth or Freedom.

Let us suppose the composer's mind filled with the sense of Beauty taking some definite form. Then that single idea in his mind generates the whole musical piece. For it first of all regulates the balance and structure of the component emotions of the piece. Each of these emotions in its turn determines the musical phrase which expresses it. The harmonies and melodies again needful for the musical phrase determine the various relations to each other of the single notes; and lastly, the single notes determine the number of air-vibrations necessary for their production. Thus the whole complex of mechanical air-vibration is generated and determined by the single idea or feeling of Beauty in the composer's mind, acting through lesser and subordinate ideas. And, *vice versâ*, the public listening to the complex of air-vibrations is led up again step by step to the realisation of and participation in that same root-idea which from the beginning was responsible for its generation.

Whoever clearly follows this concatenation and subordination of Ideas and their creative power, has already come a long way towards understanding, not only the generation of a musical piece, but the generation and creation of all nature and human life.

For the instant a new Idea or synthesis is manifested, say in the mind of a child (and the instant can often be observed), or in an adult mind—whether it be the simple idea of number, or of harmony, or of truth, or what not—it determines both observation and action: it guides as to what we shall perceive and as to how we shall act. Take the sense of Order coming to a child. The moment of this happening may often be noticed—the new perception of what order means, and the new *feeling* of pleasure in it. The two together constitute the idea of order. And at once the child sees new facts in the world around it, and arranges its life and belongings anew.

Thus again if the idea of Justice is present among a people—though it may be but a sentiment at first and on its inner side, yet quickly on its outer side it gives itself structure, and regulates the conflicting desires and emotions and needs of the people; and these emotions and desires so regulated from above do each of them in their turn generate and regulate groups of habits and customs; and these again each in their turn innumerable individual acts. And so the idea of Justice becomes creative and alive throughout the whole State.

Plato, as is well known, gave to Ideas in some such sense as this the greatest import. They existed before the world, and the world was created after their pattern (see the "Timæus"). And we can see, from what has already been said, that they are somehow implicit in the Ego before all experience. As they descend into operation and consciousness within the Man, they shape his life and form, and through him again the outer world. Thus there is a point in evolution undoubtedly when the thought and feeling of selfness emerges in the child or the monkey, or another point when the idea of courage dawns on the early man or the growing boy; and instantly in each case we see what immense vistas of life, and forms of life and action, what different ramifications and institutions of society, proceed from one such inner birth.

With Plato the great ruling Ideas were Justice, Temperance, Beauty, and the like. But he also considered that there were ideas or patterns, eternal in the heavens, of all tribes and creatures in the world, as of trees, animals, men, and the lesser gods; and he even went so far as to suppose ideas of things made by man's artifice, such as beds and tables (see "Republic," Book X.). Certainly it sounds a little comic at first to hear the "absolute essential Bed" spoken of, and Plato has been considerably berated by many folk for his daring in this matter. He has been accused of confounding the idea of a bed with the *concept* of a bed; it has been said too that if there are ideas of beds and tables, trees and animals, there must also be archetypes in heaven of pots and pans—absolutely essential worms, beetles and toadstools, and so forth. Plato, however, had no doubt considered these difficulties, and it may be worth while for our purpose to pause a moment over them.

If it were the mere *concept* of a bed, it would

of course be absurd to give it any essential reality. For the concept is a mere intellectual abstraction derived from the perception of a great number of actual beds, and is certainly *less* real than the things of which it is, so to speak, a rough sketch. But the Idea, as we have said, though it may have intellectual structure on its outer side, is on its inner side essentially a feeling. It is the feeling of Bed which constitutes the Idea, and is creative. Now in Man there is essentially such a feeling—a need and desire of sleep and the horizontal position. How deep this feeling may root in the nature of Man it might be hard to say, but we can see that it is very, very profound. And from it spring all imaginable actual beds, of most various shape and construction, yet all in their ways adapted and giving form to that feeling.

I say the idea of Bed in this sense is rooted most deep and far back in the nature of Man. But Man himself and his nature is rooted deep in the nature of God, from whom he springs—and so may we not say that in some sense the idea of Bed is rooted in the ultimate reality and nature of things?

When we see how things like beds and tables and houses may thus spring from needs or ideas, like Rest and Shelter, lying deep in the very constitution of man, it is not difficult to see further how the forms of man's body, and of the animals and trees and worms and beetles and toadstools, may have been (to a large extent) determined and created by the feelings or ideas slumbering within these beings. At some point the *feeling* of pleasure and safety in arboreal life lent form and outline to the whole race of prehensile monkeys; at some other point the sweet sensation of contrast between the moist darkness of the earth and the sunlit air of heaven gave birth to the vast tribe of vegetable beings, for ever seeking by upward and downward ramifications to extend the glad interchange between the two worlds. That these creative feelings did not appear to the individual animals and vegetables concerned as vast and luminous "Ideas," but only as dim semi-conscious desires, does not affect the argument that in this way creation has been effected. Nor do I wish to say that this is quite the way in which Plato conceives the subject. It is more like the conception of Schopenhauer. But anyhow it is an attempt to show how the Platonic ideas may be brought into some sort of line and harmony with modern science and philosophy. And it enables us dimly to see how the great panorama of creation has come forth, ever determining and manifesting itself from within through the disclosure from point to point and from time to time of ever-new creative feelings or ideas—the whole forming an immense hierarchy, culminating in the grandest, most universal, Being and Life.

Here, in the contemplation of this universal Being, this primal Self of all, we are at the source of Creation. In this primal Self, and its first differentiation, we may suppose to exist great primitive Ideas, attitudes, aspects—things below or more fundamental than Feeling, which yet work out into Feeling, Thought, and Action. These ideas are working everywhere — in the great Self, and in every lesser self that springs therefrom; and our lives *are* their expression (differently mingled though they be in each person, and always, owing to the conflict of existence, *inadequately* expressed). In quite inorganic Nature, we still perceive ideas of a certain class pervading matter, like Attraction or Repulsion, Rigidity or Fluidity, Rest or Motion, which (as we have noticed before) answer to feelings which we have within ourselves. In more organic Nature we recognise Life, Sensitiveness, Selfness, Affection; and in our fellow-man ideas of Courage, Justice, Beauty, and so forth. Everywhere in Creation we see ideas working which answer more or less to those within ourselves; and it is this answering of one to the other, of the outer to the inner, which forms the very ground of all Science and Art, and the joy that we feel in Truth and Beauty.

But in the Race too, as well as in the individual, these ideas are working; and, in fact, it is through the Race largely that they gradually gain their form and expression. This consideration must detain us a moment, as it is important.

The *feelings* which are an essential part of Ideas may be innate in the human mind, and the capacity for them may be universal, but the *forms* corresponding may vary greatly from race to race. The feeling of number, or of melody, or of justice, may be universal in mankind; but the arithmetical systems, or the diatonic scales, or the social institutions of the various races may be very various. The abstract feeling of number then, or of melody, or of justice, may correspond to the Idea of Plato, formless in the heavens, or in the bosom of God; but when it comes to take form in the various races of mankind it does so with variety, according to the necessity of outward circumstances, and the genius and tradition of each race. Thus Plato feigns in the "Timæus" that the universal spirit of God handed over the seeds of the immortal, imperishable Ideas to the lesser gods, who, each according to the race of men or animals over which he presided, was to embody these seeds in external forms. Thus the various races of living creatures arose—all vivified from within by the eternal Ideas, yet all having their various structures according to their races, and the genius of the particular god presiding over the race.

In the language of modern Science, using the term "Heredity" to cover much the same ground as "the genius of the race-god," we should say that while the ideas (say of melody and of flight in the case of birds) are the vivifying impulses of any class of creatures, the particular forms (as of songs and of wings) are a matter of slowly growing heredity and the tradition of the race.

Let us take the example of Courage in man.

At a certain stage in evolution, doubtless, the idea of Courage dawned on primitive Man. He may have fought in a scrambling, spasmodic way before that, but without any nucleus to his ardour. Now round this new idea, this new sense, a distinct life grew. He admired courage in others, he strove for it in himself. And it took form. The idea (which in the abstract, or in heaven, may be formless enough) took form—and became embodied in a certain type of man, according to the race, according to its tradition, according to its needs and environment. The physical and moral type of courage in the mind of a Greek (the dress, the figure, the temperament, the character) would be very different from that in the mind of a North American Indian; and that again from the type in the mind of a modern soldier: the *form* depending on more or less traceable external conditions, but the feeling being one which comes to all races and men at a certain stage of growth.

Thus Heredity comes in. The ancestors having all been accustomed to associate Courage with a certain type of man and action, we can hardly doubt that in some way (*pace* Weismann) the repeated impressions cohere in the descendant, or at least leave the descendant mind the more ready to respond to that particular type; till in the course of centuries and thousands of years, a particular form rouses a particular feeling with the greatest intensity, or, on the other hand, a feeling calls up a particular form. The modern boy sees in a red-coat soldier an emblem of superhuman valour, when a befeathered Apache brave would only fill him with contempt and ridicule. Thus the creative Idea, through heredity and individual experience combined, works in this or that form in this or that race—though in the course of centuries, with changing circumstances or development, the form too may slowly change.

Or we may take the example of Love—how of this inner feeling a certain external type of Woman (owing to the genius and heredity and circumstances of the race) may become the emblem and ideal, how this type may figure as the goddess of Love for the race, and become a great power in the midst of it. Or again Justice—how certain institutions getting ingrained by heredity in race-habit, as associated with this sentiment, acquire a great sacredness and authority, and are most difficult to alter—though to other races or folk they may seem quite horrible. Or even of beds and tables—how the idea of a bed in one race may work itself out in a ponderous four-poster, and in another in a simple mat on the ground, and in a third in the form of a hammock. Though the feeling and the need of Sleep may be practically the same in all races, yet the forms and structures in which it finds expression may be so different as to be almost meaningless and useless to those unaccustomed to them.

Thus we get a glimpse of great formative ideas lying even behind the evolution of races, and largely guiding these evolutions (subject of course to external influences, and such things as the clashing of the ideas of one race with those of another); and we see how the expression of ideas, through the long race-life and the repetition of them in the same form, may gain an extraordinary intensity—a subject to which we shall return in the next chapter. We see too in what way Plato was justified in saying that the Ideas were the real things and the mundane objects only illusive forms. For clearly the hammock and the mat and the four-poster, and all the countless variations of these are, none of them, the absolute essential Bed or Bedness—but rather this term must be applied to that profound quality of man's nature from which all mortal beds proceed. And clearly all the horribly discordant law-books and laws and law-courts and prisons are none of them Justice; but this term must be applied to that deep sentiment of which all these are the lame expression. "For nothing can have any sense except by reason of that of which it is the shadow." And finally, we may ask whether for a true understanding of the trees and the plants and the animals we must not refer them in a similar way to the root-ideas and feelings from which they spring, and of which they strive to be the expression.

To recapitulate. The creative source is in the transcendent Self of all things. This Self at its first differentiation into multiplex 'aspects' (or individualities) manifests at the same time the Ideas which are inherent in its being;[1] and these again descend into Feeling, Thought, and Action, and finally into external structure and life—which latter may be looked upon as largely due to the conditioning or limitation of the ideas manifested in one individuality by those manifested in another. Anyhow, we can see that the manifestation takes place under certain external conditions, and that by the time it descends into actual structure it has been largely swayed by those conditions. These external forms built up in any race for the manifestation or expression of Ideas are riveted and emphasised by Heredity (or by the hammering of the race-god through the centuries), and acquire an extraordinary sanctity and transcendent glamour through this process, so that the mere appearance of the form instantly wakes the Idea or deep transcendent feeling which belongs to it. Thus we come near to Plato's ἀνάμνησις, and see how a kind of memory of celestial visions and powers may be roused by the sight of mortal things.

We see too that the self of one race, having branched off somewhere from the primal Self,

[1] It is not difficult to see how the very first differentiation of the One into the Multiple must necessarily mean the manifestation of certain great primal Ideas—such as Union (or love), Individuality (or pride), Equality, Justice, Power (the life of the Many in the One), Beauty (the beholding of the One in the Many), Truth, and so forth. The Ideas have no force or validity of their own except as inherent in the primal Being or in those beings affiliated to it; and Being has no differentiation except through the Ideas which it manifests.

may embody or manifest the Ideas in somewhat different degree or different order, say from the self of another race; and again that the individual Ego branching from the race-Ego—though it carries on the general forms and ideas of the race—may manifest them in different degree or combination from another individual. Yet it has to be remembered that the absolute self of the individual *is* still ultimately the transcendent World-self (coming down in time through the Race-self, but by no means necessarily tied to the race-forms), and that the individual, notwithstanding his heredity, has still an access and appeal to a region and powers beyond and prior to all heredity.

VIII

THE GODS AS APPARITIONS OF THE RACE-LIFE

We are now in a position to understand in some degree the mysterious figures of the gods—those figures which, clothed with dominion and terror, or with grace and beauty, have hovered like phantoms for thousands and scores of thousands of years over the earlier races of the Earth.

When we look back at the wonderful panorama of them—at the timeless gods of Egypt, the strange mesmeric gods of India, the just yet merciful Judges of Assyria, the gracious deities of Greece, the warlike, restless powers of Scandinavia, the fateful, terrible gods of Mexico, and all the grotesque, half-brute, half-human idols of countless savage races; or even at the deities and saints of the Christian Church, the Virgin Mary, the Holy Ghost, the infant or the crucified Christ, and the lesser figures grouped round them in the Catholic Heaven—the question cannot but force itself on us: What is the meaning of it all? What gave to these figures their intense reality and significance for the people over whom they presided?

For although modern Science has tackled this

question, and although we feel that the current explanations which it gives are suggestive—as of generalisations of Nature-phenomena, anthropomorphic superstitions, idealisations of heroic men and women, and so forth, modified by traditions and memories and dreams, and complicated by mistakes in the meanings of words and names—we feel also that these explanations fail almost entirely to account for the astounding power and influence of the figures concerned, or to reveal why to the savage and untutored mind mere traditions and generalisations and abstractions should have acquired such intense reality.

For no one can consider the subject for a moment without seeing that for each race its gods were (at any rate in the earlier period of their apparition) actually existent beings. When we read that Pheidippides, having been sent by the Athenians to Sparta to ask for aid against the Persians, was exhausted by the way (for he covered, it was said, the one hundred and fifty miles in less than two days), and that as he rested for a moment in some quiet valley beside a spring, lo! the great god Pan appeared to him, and his voice was heard promising victory to the Athenians; and further, that the latter in consequence dedicated a temple to Pan after the battle of Marathon, and honoured him thenceforth with annual sacrifices and a torch-race—we cannot but feel that whatever was the actual occurrence, the popular belief in the reality of the apparition and the voice was irresistible. Or when in the Homeric epos Athené comes from the sky and takes Achilles by his yellow hair, and the wrathful hero, at the behest of her terribly brilliant eyes, sheathes his sword; or when in the Ramáyana the supreme god Krishna, in the form of the charioteer, holds long discourse with Arjuna on the field of battle, speaking words of eternal and divine wisdom,—we see that though these incidents may be literary inventions, they derive all their force from the fact that they would appeal to an immense and wide-spread conviction that such incidents could and did occur. Or when we come to comparatively modern witnesses, like Saint Francis, who beheld the Madonna descend from the sky and place in his arms her Divine Son, or Catherine of Siena, for whom Heaven opened and showed her the Christ sitting upon the Throne; or consider hundreds and hundreds of similar stories, and how the presence and activity and profound influence of such figures and beings have been admitted and accepted and insisted on by millions and millions of human kind in all races and in all ages; and the belief in them has compelled men to every conceivable heroism and devotion, and terror of death and sacrifice—it is impossible, I say, not to see how intense was the reality with which they were credited, and difficult not to suppose that (whatever these apparitions actually were) they represented some real force or forces influencing mankind.

After what has been said in preceding chapters

it may be guessed what my answer would be to these questions. It is that these figures derive their profound influence from the fact that they represent the *life of the race itself*; that they are the manifestation and expression of that life, of which (as far as our bodies are concerned) we are offshoots and affiliations—so that through them we reach to *another and more extended order of consciousness*, we partake of a vaster life, and are correspondingly deeply moved. If we look upon the vast race-life as the manifestation of one great aspect of the World-Self or Ego, and on the great formative Ideas of the race as its gods, whose essence is eternal but whose *form* (as we saw in the last chapter) is apparitional and dependent in some degree on outer circumstances; then we can understand how through these forms we may enter into the race-life and the great Ideas that inspire it, and come one step nearer to the world-self. We may be lifted for a moment out of our work-a-day existence and touch upon that which is eternal.

For the moment I only wish to suggest this general answer—and even so I do not wish to limit the answer too much, or say that it is *only* through the race-life that we reach a higher order of consciousness. But certainly through the race-consciousness much may come; and it may be worth while to consider it more in detail.

In studying any phenomenon of the past it is always advisable to try and detect it in the life of to-day. And the moment we do so in this case we see that the gods are still living and real all around us. Allowing all one may for mere cant or custom, yet there are thousands and thousands round us to whom the figure of Christ, say, is an intense, a living, and an actually present reality. It is difficult to suppose that all these people are merely deceiving themselves. One must see that whatever this figure is, or proceeds from, it is much more than the imagination of a fairy tale, and represents a real power there present and acting within the man. It is a thing of the same character as the deities of olden time.

Or again, who is there so unfortunate as not to have had the experience, in ordinary daily life, of seeing some features, perhaps those of a well-known person, suddenly transformed into the lineaments of a god—with the strangest possible sense of a transcendent Presence, only to be described by some such word? Or why, on occasions, walking along the crowded streets amid all the rubbish and riff-raff of humanity, does a face suddenly appear, all glorified and shining, removed by a measureless gulf from those around—and disappear again in the stream? What is the meaning of these sudden halos and glamours?

Dr. Bucke, in his "Memories of Walt Whitman," describes the profound impression produced upon him by his first interview with the poet. "I remember well how, like so many others, I was struck, almost amazed, by the beauty and majesty of his person and the gracious air of purity that surrounded and permeated him. We did not talk much, nor do I remember anything that was said, but it would be impossible for me to fully convey by words or in any way to describe the influence upon me of that short and simple interview. A sort of spiritual intoxication set in, which did not reach its culmination for several weeks, and which, after continuing for some months, very gradually, in the course of the next few years, faded out. While this state of exaltation remained at its height the mental image of the man Walt Whitman underwent within me a sort of glorification (or else a veil was withdrawn and I saw him as he was and is), insomuch that it became impossible for me (I am describing the event just as it occurred, and as accurately as possible) to believe that Whitman was a mere man. It seemed to me at that time certain that he was either *actually a god or in some sense clearly and entirely preterhuman.* Be all this as it may, it is certain that the hour spent that day with the poet was the turning-point of my life." These words of Dr. Bucke are specially interesting as coming from no sentimental youth, but from a man of scientific and practical attainment who at the time of the recorded experience was fully forty years old, and superintendent of a large insane asylum; and they show clearly enough his deliberate conviction that he beheld in Whitman the presence of a being divine and beyond the range of mortality.

Or again, we ask, why do the mountain-peaks

and the thunder-clouds sometimes take on a mystic light, and stir us with a sense of something unearthly? Why in the sylvan glades do we become aware, perhaps quite unexpectedly, of a breathless stillness and magic, and the trees stand as though the Wood-god himself were there, and the air exhales a mystery? What is this light which never was on sea or land? We see that these things are realities in the sense that they so deeply influence us. We surmise that they are something more than phantoms or fictions of our own individual brains.

I have already touched upon the effort of Plato to explain these mysteries. Plato believed in a world of Absolute Forms and Essences remaining beyond the reach of Time. There, in company with the gods, dwelt—and for ever dwell—Justice and Temperance and Beauty and many other Ideas. The soul of every man in some earlier state of being, carried round in the retinue of that special god to whom he may belong, has beheld in that heavenly world these divine Essences. But fallen now to Earth it has wellnigh forgotten them. Only now and then, when the man sees some fair face or figure, witnesses some heroic deed or well-balanced action, or even perceives some well-formed object, is he *reminded* of that which is Eternal. For Plato the explanation of the Divine was easy enough. It was an ἀνάμνησις—a recollection, faint or powerful, of things once known and seen. When you set eyes—might Plato say—upon that face in the crowd it was not so much the face itself that was divine (though it was certainly privileged so far to resemble divinity), but that it instantly recalled to your memory the form of some god seen long ago, or far down in the mirror of the mind—to which god indeed your adoration and worship were due, and not to the mortal; or if to the mortal, only so far as in him (or her) the image of the god were faintly visible. Of these celestial forms (and these are Plato's actual words in the "Phædrus") "few only retain an adequate remem brance; and they, when they behold any image of that other world, are rapt in amazement; but they are ignorant of what this rapture means, because they do not clearly perceive. *For there is no light in the earthly copies* of justice or temperance or any of the higher qualities which are precious to souls: they are seen through a glass dimly; and there are few who, going to the images, behold in them the realities, and they only with difficulty." Thus for Plato the explanation of "the light which never was on sea or land" was easy enough. It was a memory of that celestial light in which the divine Ideas and heavenly beings themselves were once seen by the soul; and indeed are (according to him) ever seen, whenso it may succeed in penetrating into that region where they dwell eternal.

We have seen (in the last chapter) how it may be possible to look upon this theory of Plato's in the light of modern science and philosophy. The Ideas, we saw, on their inner and essential side are states of being, states of feeling. It is on their outer side that they take form and structure. So that ultimately the mundane forms in which they express themselves may not only be very various (several or many forms being capable of expressing one idea), but the mundane forms are also necessarily imperfect expressions, and largely determined by external accident and circumstance. We saw also how Heredity in the race comes in to stamp and accentuate the connection between a comparatively imperfect and accidental form, and the Idea which it represents—and to such a degree that at last the mere momentary sight of the said imperfect form may wake the Idea, or state of being and feeling, with the greatest intensity. Thus a real *ἀνάμνησις* takes place—that is, a remembrance or revivifying of divine things in the mind through a mere external phenomenon. The countless memories of the race, all associated for generations with the particular object—or the sum and result of these memories—wake the Idea in the mind of the present individual with a seemingly supernatural force. Let us go into this subject yet more closely.

We all know that the young of animals act in a way which suggests that their psychical selves, their memory and experience, are in some way continuous with those of their ancestors. Young partridges, or the chicks of the barndoor fowl, only a day old, at sight of any large bird in the air, will instantly and instinctively crouch and flatten themselves on the ground. Their alarm, increased by the warning call of the mother, causes them to seek refuge under her wings. What definite form the sense of danger takes in the young chick's mind it is of course hard to say. But there it seems to be—the memory of a thousand and a hundred thousand occasions in the history of the chick's ancestors, when the dreaded claws and beak came from the sky and snatched or nearly snatched the cowering prey. So clear and oft-repeated has the association become, that now the Vision of a bird above governs, so to speak, a whole plexus of nerves, not only in the chick, but even in the adult partridge or fowl, and sets in movement, almost automatically, a whole apparatus of muscles of defence or flight. The certainty and instantaneousness with which this happens is something astonishing. Personally I am never tired of watching my barndoor fowls on the occasions when the sweep comes to clean the chimney. On the moment when the brush emerges from the top of the chimney—whatever the fowls are doing, whether they are feeding or basking, or foraging in far grounds—in that instant with shrieks and screams they rush in every direction seeking for cover: convinced that an awful enemy has appeared on the roof. A cap thrown high in the air has the same effect. It is not that a cap in form or movement is so very like a bird (in fact, some of my fowls must know well enough in their hearts exactly what my cap really is), but that it wakes the latent remembrance of the bird of prey. The fowls do not really see the cap or the chimney sweep's brush, but they see what may be called the Vision of the Ideal Hawk — *which is far stronger and more deeply embedded in their very physiology* than any momentary image can be, and has a far more powerful influence on them.

All this is quite like the Platonic reminiscence. We do not really see the rather commonplace features which pass in the street, but some celestial vision (in the race-consciousness) of which they remind us; and it is this latter which agitates and transports us. At the back of our eyes, so to speak, and in the profound depths of the race-life (of which each individual is but a momentary point) is stored the remote past of the world; and through our eyes look the eyes of dead ancestors. Thus we see not merely the bare object, but rather it is surrounded by a strange halo and glamour, which is the presence of all this past.

Let us take an important and definite instance from human life. In the last chapter we spoke of Courage. In the history of nations War is of supreme importance; and we can see how the Idea of the hero, or courageous warrior, has helped to build up every race. Working in the race through the centuries, and under certain external conditions, it has produced a certain type of warriors. Of these warriors some naturally would be more representative and efficient than others, and these would be the mighty men of valour to whom every one would look up. Among early and warlike races, probably far the greater part of the activity of the male portion of the race, and of the love-longing of the female portion, has thus clustered round the figure of the mighty warrior. The man who towers head and shoulders above his fellows, who is a terror to his enemies and a fortress of strength to his friends, necessarily occupies a commanding position in the minds of those around him, be they friends or foes—especially in the minds of the youth. His image is the object of their admiration and emulation, it is associated with the most thrilling exploits, it is the symbol of all they would desire to be, in themselves or their children. Every young man has had two or three such figures stamped on his brain; between which figures there will doubtless be some degree of similarity, and some degree of blending into a joint ideal.

But (and this is the important point) the same process has been taking place through the generations; and going back through the long succession of any one line of ancestry we seem to see that countless images have been imprinted (each with great intensity in its time) and superimposed on one another—the result being the formation of a great composite form or symbol, which, slowly altering, will be inherited by each descendant, and will lie there, perhaps for a long time slumbering and unbeknown to the individual, at the centre of all the emotions and activities concerned in warfare and patriotism, and associated with some nerve-plexus which governs these activities and affections in the human body.[1]

This composite then, like a composite photograph of many faces upon the same plate, will not show individual details and variations except by implication, but rather the large outlines of the group which it represents—in this case the warrior-hero. In the hundreds and thousands of images which go to form it, defects, disproportions, inharmonious details, will cancel each other out, and there will emerge a Form, harmonious, grand, and not far from perfect—the warrior-god, in fact, of the race—the result, so to speak, of the selection and chiselling of thousands of minds through the centuries.

But if in one sense this God-form is the result of the chiselling of thousands of minds, in another it is the Form which the Heroic Idea working through the centuries has fashioned for itself and has inspired the multitudinous minds to adore. It is the god himself, as one aspect of the race-life, whom we here see in his double activity—both as producing certain types of manhood, and as inspiring others to reverence and store in memory these types, so that at last

[1] If it sounds too crude and materialistic to speak of an inherited composite image as dwelling in or associated with a nerve-plexus, yet we must allow that by heredity the nerves become adjusted so as to respond to images of a certain class or composite type. And if again our knowledge of nerve-plexuses is too uncertain yet to show exactly how ideas and emotions are associated with them, yet that there is some such general association is for the most part admitted by the modern psychologists and physiologists.

through the mortal types the god himself may be beheld, and the race-life and race-consciousness entered into. There in its appropriate centre or nerve-structure of the human body the heroic Idea dwells, inspiring the blended memory of countless heroic actions, feats of bravery, struggles, defeats, triumphs, and so forth, and governing in the individual man the vast congregation of powers and activities with which it is concerned. No wonder that when the sight of a living warrior wakes this slumbering centre within the youth, devotion and emulation, excitement and the ardour of heroic deeds, for him can know no bounds.

Let us take another instance. There is no class of mental impressions much more powerful and persistent through all time than those connected with the relation of the sexes. For ages, thousands of centuries, the Male has sought the Female, the Female has sought the Male. Here we are at the very centre and focus of race-life. Love, in this sense, means union of differentiated and opposing elements, by which the balance of race-life is restored, and the self or Being who is at the root of this life comes one step farther to manifestation. This Titanic being, who through the ages (and always working subject to some external conditions) has thrown out multitudinous types, always more or less imperfect, of itself, dwells also hidden within each individual. Not only metaphysically speaking does it dwell in each individual, but through the long process of Heredity, its Form or Forms (the race-ideals or race-gods) lie slumbering there[1]—and in closest touch with all the nerve-structures and potencies which have to do with the generation of the race. Then come together two individuals whose opposite polarities and differentiations will together build an adequate expression, and instantly in each other they wake this Titanic life, and the god-figures belonging to it. The youth sees the girl; it may be a chance face, a chance outline, amid the most banal surroundings. But it gives the cue. There is a memory, a confused reminiscence. The mortal figure without penetrates to the immortal figure within; and there rises into consciousness a shining Form, glorious, not belonging to this world, but vibrating with the agelong life of humanity, and the memory of a thousand love-dramas. The waking of this vision intoxicates the man; it glows and burns within him; a goddess (it may be Venus herself) stands in the sacred place of his Temple; a sense of awe-struck splendour fills him; and the world is changed.[2]

"He whose initiation is recent," says Plato,

[1] As in the case of the Warrior-god, we may imagine that every man inherits from his countless male ancestors a susceptibility to a certain type of feminine beauty; and every woman from her female ancestors a susceptibility to a certain ideal of manhood.

[2] The *degree* in which this Form comes into clear Vision may vary much with different races or individuals. In many cases a distinct vision is never realised, though it may be indicated by the agitation and excitement felt, and by the halo thrown round the mortal creature. Anyhow, it must be remembered (what we have already said) that the Idea on its inner side is a state of being or feeling, and only on its outer and less essential side a form. Aristotle calls the Platonic Ideas *αἰσθητὰ ἀΐδια.*

"and who has been spectator of many glories in the other world, is amazed when he sees any one having a god-like face or form, which is the expression of Divine Beauty; and at first a shudder runs through him, and again the old awe steals over him; then looking upon the face of his beloved as of a god he reverences him, and if he were not afraid of being thought a downright madman, he would sacrifice to his beloved as to the image of a god." And Lafcadio Hearn, who in his "Out of the East" and in his "Exotics and Retrospectives" has written much that is suggestive on this point, says this visionary figure is "a composite of numberless race-memories . . . a beautiful luminous ghost made of centillions of memories"; but he adds, somewhat in the spirit of Thomas Hardy, "you will now remember the beloved seemed lovelier than mortal woman could be."

In truth, as we have said before, the mortal object which wakes the ideal in our minds, and the Ideal itself, though occasionally confused, are on the whole clearly distinct and separable in thought from each other. *They are perceived by separate faculties.* The object, so far as it is a mortal object, is perceived by the senses, by surface sight and touch and hearing; but not so the inner Vision. Plato says that this state of mind, in which Divine Beauty is seen (and which is associated with all real love), is a "Mania," and that only in this condition of "Mania" can the heavenly facts be perceived or remembered.

What he seems to indicate by this—and what we, in modern speech, should probably say—is that it is another *state of consciousness* which is concerned: that is, that while the objects of the outer world are perceived by us through the senses, co-ordinated under the conditions of the ordinary consciousness, these ancient (race) memories, and the feelings and visions which come with them, belong to another order of consciousness. Indeed, it almost seems obvious that it must be so. If the existence of race-memories, and of feelings and visions accompanying them, is allowed at all, it would seem that these things must belong in some degree to the consciousness of the race, to a less individual and local consciousness than the ordinary one. The terms 'mania,' then, or 'ecstasy,' which would indicate the passing out from the ordinary consciousness (into the racial or celestial, according as we adopt the modern or Platonic view), would seem quite appropriate.

There is one other point just here. I say the outer object and the Ideal Memory which it wakes in the mind, though separable in thought, are for a time confused with one another. The splendours of the Ideal are showered upon and invest the object. Yet dimly the mind feels that it *is* remembering something, and wonders to what previous experience the object is akin. Is this the explanation of that curious sense of Familiarity, at first sight, which is so often excited by the idealisation of another person?

A memory is indeed awakened, and of a figure most intimate to oneself, but slumbering deep in the recesses of one's own mind.

Going back to the subject of the Warrior, we see that Hero-worship is not confined to that form. Worship of the Athlete, the Saint, the King, come under the same head. In modern Europe as in ancient Greece, the Athlete excites the mad enthusiasm of crowds. In India, as in mediæval Europe, romance and idealism gather at least as strongly round the Saint. These are matters of race and temperament. Everywhere, with the exception of a few peoples who have advanced beyond this stage, the King is granted divine honours. No one can witness the excitement produced by Royalty without perceiving that it is an instinct, like that of bees for their Queen—that is, a *race*-consciousness or sentiment. The glamour is that of an Idea, an Ideal King, a figure composite in the memory of the race, and the centre of its agelong hopes and fears and growth and struggle and conquest, and the glamour is readily and easily transferred to the living and actual representative, however unworthy he may be. Almost every one recognises that it is so. The word "King" spoken to an Englishman wakens in his conscious mind a conjoint image of a succession of sovereigns from Alfred say to Edward VII.; but to his *subconscious self* it means far far more than that. It means an epitome of the devotion, the fear, the awe, the confidence which every one of his ancestors felt towards the ruler of his day, and that not only as far back as Alfred, but into the almost unending past, when the relation of every man to his chieftain was far closer than now—all this mighty mass of feeling concentrated in one great Vision of Kinghood, one instinct of devoted Service. It is obvious that this mass of feeling being still there, and still centred and co-ordinated in that particular way, it must pour itself out at some time, and the particular Royalty of the day is only the excuse, as it were, for such outpouring.

But from this perception of a glow or halo round the figure of a king to his transformation into a god is but a short step. The actual mortal sovereign is identified with the immortal, ever-abiding race-memory and the idealised figure of Kinghood which dwells there. Everywhere we see this taking place. The Egyptian Pharaohs were exalted into gods. To the Roman Cæsars temples were built and divine honours paid. The Aztec and Peruvian emperors the same. Even to-day, for the Russian peasant or the tribesman of Morocco, the glamour of absolute deity surrounds the Tsar or the Sultan.

IX

THE GODS AS DWELLING IN THE PHYSIOLOGICAL CENTRES

I INDICATED in the last chapter how the form and figure of the actual king may rise into that of a god through its blending with the immense subconscious emotion of the race. So of other gods and divinities The idealisation of the Warrior growing through successive generations obscurely but powerfully in the primitive Latin folk, suddenly—perhaps through the appearance of an actual man who fulfilled the ideal to an extraordinary degree—may have taken definite shape and name in the figure of Mars; who thenceforth, identified with the ideal, stood as the God of War for succeeding time. Or the enthusiasm for the Athlete or strong man, so deeply rooted in primitive peoples, may have been brought to a focus by the appearance of a real Heracles or Hercules. The names and figures, then, of these men, became for after generations the centre of this enthusiasm and deep racial instinct of admiration, and to these names were ascribed many exploits, not only of these, but of other heroes before and after. And since in any such cases of mighty men appearing among a people, the exploits which would produce the most profound impression would be those which were most beneficial to the folk—the slaying of monsters and wild beasts, the cleansing of pestilent swamps, the taming of oxen, the wrestling with death, and so forth—so it would be these which would be enshrined in the public memory, and which (from various sources) would cluster round the ideal figure of the Hero or Saviour.

This myth-making tendency of races, and the unconscious clustering of incidents and anecdotes from various sources round one or more definite figures, is of course well recognised, and explains how it is these legends often seem to contain so deep a sentiment and meaning. It is that they are the selection and affectionate preservation from the memorial life of the race of events and stories which illustrate and symbolise some deep instinct and enthusiasm of the race; such stories being gradually and unconsciously modified into more and more of expressiveness as time goes on. In this way many great epic poems, legends, myths, and traditions of the gods have been built up. And such things have inevitably a profound sentiment in them. They are wiser than any one man could make them—for they represent the feelings, the enthusiasms, the wonderments, the humour, the wit, the activities to which the race has responded for generations. If such legends and stories were merely *mental* ideals, if they were such handy little allegories and generalisations as any philosopher or literary person might make in his study, they would be very cheap and paltry affairs. The whole point of the argument will be missed unless it is seen that the Ideas and enthusiasms which produce myths and legends lie deep down in the very structure and physical organisation of humanity, and in its very *physiology*—that they are things of agelong life and importance, principalities and powers (if we may so call them) which in the form of these legends and figures are slowly rising into recognition, but which belong to another order of existence, so to speak, than that with which we are usually concerned.

Here is another god, Mercury—to whom among the Greeks Hermes corresponds, and who is represented also among other nations—the Swift runner, the Messenger-god. It seems a little curious at first that a mere messenger-ideal should be deified. Where did the glow or glamour which transformed him come from? But when you consider what the swift runner really represented in those days—when you think for a moment what the postal service, the telegraph, the locomotive, and all the other means of intercommunication are to *us*—when you think of the story of Pheidippides mentioned above, a people in its agony sending their fleetest foot-racer to the neighboring state for help, and of the profound sensation, the tears of joy, the enthusiasm, the worship, with which he would be greeted on his return; then it is easy to see that round the figure of the Messenger generally in the national consciousness a glamour would grow which would easily transform such figure into a god. And as swift communication means many things beside the delivery of messages—as it means the growth of commerce, the coming into contact with strange peoples and languages and so forth—so the Messenger god, Hermes, or Mercury, or Thoth, or whoever he might be, would not only be the deliverer of divine messages, but would stand for the patron of all interpretations, mysteries, travel, and commerce (and so even of thieving).

The goddess of Love and of feminine grace and beauty, Aphrodite, Venus, Freia, Astarte, is one to whom we have already referred. Her temples and worship have been honoured among almost all races. We need not go again over ground which we have already partly covered. That there is among the nerves of the human body, of the brain and of the great sympathetic system, some kind of centre or plexus, or group of plexuses, which co-ordinates and dominates the love-instinct, and that this is one of the most powerful and important centres in the body; that connected and associated with this centre and its ramifications is a whole world of emotions, desires, mental images, thoughts, activities; and that this centre, in both its physical and mental aspects, is the result and growth and embodiment of centuries and ages of race-experience—these are things that few will deny.

And that the successive images of feminine form and feature acting on this centre in long hereditary line may have combined to one powerful joint Impression—which, even though latent in consciousness, dominates and moves all the race-memories of love—is something which seems at least very probable.[1]

The raising of this Composite, this luminous ghost, into consciousness, in the history of a race, is in this view the creation or birth of the Goddess of Love, for that race. Love itself existed from immemorial time; but when into it a deeper consciousness began to come, it was filled with strange force and fire, an extraordinary glow and glamour, and a vague sense of divinity and of a life beyond the moment; and when, beyond that, the race-consciousness itself in some moment of inspiration awoke, bringing the astounding revelation of its own memory, like a fairy mountain peak rising over the world, then the individual beheld the veritable Goddess, and divined that Love was immortal.

It will, perhaps, be said that though this way of looking at the matter may account for those

[1] It is important to remember, in this connection, that in all the great plexuses of the Sympathetic Nerve-system there ramify not only the nerve-fibres of the Sympathetic itself, but also nerve-fibres from the cerebro-spinal system and nerve-fibres from the cerebrum. We thus have in the case of each plexus, and brought together into one focus, capacities of immense emotional agitation (the Sympathetic), capacities of swift reflex action and response (the cerebro-spinal), and the formation of powerful mental images (the cerebrum). These three elements cannot well be separated from each other, and working together in any centre they represent a kind of dæmonic presence.

gods which are idealisations of human types, it does not explain why the mere things of Nature, like the Moon and the Sun, or the Darkness and the Dawn, should be personified. But the least thought shows that the anthropomorphic tendency is in some degree inevitable in us. The Moon and the Sun are to us what they are, only because they have appeared in human consciousness. Consider for a moment the latter. How many millions of times has the great Sun risen on our primitive ancestors after the dark and perilous night, with unspeakable sense of joy, relief, comfort? How continually has this sense grown, with reverberant intensity in the successive generations?—till at last in some more than usually subtle or sensitive soul it has broken into a strange consciousness of a Presence—*the presence*, in fact, within that soul, *of the myriad life and emotion of those that have gone before*. The rising orb, the growing glory of the sky, have wakened a multitudinous memory—the memory and consciousness of mankind itself in its most adventurous and buoyant mood; and to this child of Man, this primitive poet, the Sun has indeed appeared as not only a circle of light in the sky, but as the symbol and reminiscent vision of a majestic and celestial being, going forth to his daily conquest of the world, hero of a thousand battles, and with the magic upon him of a life immortal.

Or, similarly, how often has Night descended, with a mystic sense of human terror, doubt, and awe, a million times distilled and concentrated? Or seriously, can even we moderns, in tall hat and patent leather boots, regard the young Moon in the clear sky of evening without a most foolish yet poignant tenderness and romance, and a sense as if within us and through our eyes sheer myriads of other eyes were watching her?

In all these cases there is a personification truly; but it is because what we are really coming into touch with is not the so-called Moon or Sun, or Darkness or Dawn, so much as the great subconscious mind of the race under its different aspects. It is in this immense world which comes down to us from the far past—that city of a thousand gates of which we in our individual bodies are but the portals, and yet into which through our bodies we have entrance—that we must look for the Gods, and for all the evidences of a life which, though greater than that we commonly call our own, belongs to us and is indeed ours.

And here we come again to the point which is the main subject of this chapter, the connection of it all with Physiology. All those deities I have mentioned—the gods and goddesses of Day and Night, the Gods of War and of Love, the Hero-god or Saviour, the King-god or Lord of heaven, and many more, represent very distinct centres and co-ordinations of feelings and activities in the race; but they also, as we have hinted, represent very distinct centres of organic life in each human body, which is indeed an epitome of the race: they represent such physiological centres as Love, Pugnacity, Sympathy, Sleep, and so forth. The gods, in fact, may be said not only to be aspects of the life of the race, but to dwell in some sense in the organic nuclei and plexuses of the body, and to be the centres of command and service there.

Strange as this may sound, it is yet most important; and the appreciation of this point gives perhaps more than anything else the key to the understanding of the religions of paganism and the past, and to the progress of humanity in the future. The body is not vile. It is not only a Temple of God, but it is a collection of temples; and just as the images of the gods dwell in the temples of a land, and are the objects of service and the centres of command there, so, we may say, the gods themselves dwell in the centres and sacred places of the body. The one thing is an allegory or symbol of the other, and it has been the instinct of primitive humanity to express itself in this way. Every organ and centre of the body is the seat of some great emotion, which in its proper activity and due proportion is truly divine. It is through this bodily and physiological centre that the emotion, the *enthusiasm*, that portion of the divine Being, expresses itself; and in the pure and perfect body that expression, that activity, is itself a revelation. The total physiology of Man is, or should be, the nearest expression of divinity complete, and the replica or image of the physiology of the Cosmos itself.

Once this conception of the relation of the human body, not only to the life of the race, but to the whole world of the emotions and inner life of Man, and to the panorama of his gods, is fairly seized and appropriated, many things become clear. And as we go on doubtless the whole subject will become clearer. At present, however, we must pass to two other points which need consideration.

In the first place, these great formative forces, Ideas, Enthusiasms, which manifest themselves in the race-life, and, clothed with emotion, dwell in the hidden centres of the actual body, are, from the nature of the case, things which we only become directly conscious of in those moments of excitement or exaltation which take us into the deeper regions of our being. Though they may be vaguely felt by the ordinary consciousness, they cannot very well be described in its terms. They are therefore only seen and seized in their fulness by the few—by the few whose more harmonious natures fit them for the vision; or if by the many, only in rare moments. And so it becomes the function of the inspired prophets, poets, artists, to give these a definite form and name—as Moses did, who bodied forth Jehovah for the Jews, or as Pheidias the sculptor is said to have finally fixed and shapen the ideal of Athenè for the Athenians. The many, when they see these forms bodied forth by the great Seers, leap to them and accept them, feeling distinctly enough that they answer to something which is slumbering within them, though they cannot quite seize the latter directly The actual figures of the Gods, in fact, accepted and adopted by the various races, cannot be said to be realities, but are rather symbols or representations, adapted to the ordinary consciousness, of real powers working in the race and profoundly moving and inspiring it.

In the second place, these real Powers (ruling in our nerve-centres as the image-gods rule in the Temples) are themselves, of course, always growing—that is to say, that as the race grows and branches, *their* forms also modify and change—slowly, indeed, through centuries, but steadily. But as the *images*—the once-inspired forms which were embodied in stone or paintings, or in holy books and ceremonials—as these do not change, so in time *they* cease to correspond to the realities, they cease to be inspired or to awaken inspiration, and become dry and dead conventions. On this subject, however, of Conventions as affecting the Gods I will say no more here. It leads to the consideration of the change in religious forms and divinities which takes place as time and history go on, and the eternal conflict between letter and spirit.[1]

Returning now to the general line of thought, I would say a few words on the subject of Christianity. In speaking of the genesis of the deities hitherto, I have dwelt more especially on the pagan gods of Greece and Rome. The appearance of Christianity on the scene marked a new

[1] See "Angels' Wings," by E. Carpenter, chap. v. (Sonnenschein).

growth—not exactly a new growth in the history of the world, because something much (though not quite) the same had appeared long before in India and Egypt—but new in the West There was growing, in the races which gathered round Imperial Rome, a sense—partly due, perhaps, to reaction from the life of the day—a sense of the presence of death, a longing for some other life, a belief in the power of gentleness, meekness, chastity—things which had been comparatively little considered by the preceding Nature-religions. It surely might almost be said that a new centre of organic life was forming—a new plexus among the nerves of Humanity. No one can visit India without being struck by what seems quite a physiological difference between the average Hindu and the average Westerner—the passivity of the former, the mildness, the meekness, the meditative transcendental temper, the sense of another world, the little fear of death. His organism seems to be differently keyed from ours; so that while the Anglo-Saxon masses are shouting themselves hoarse over a football hero or other Athlete, the Hindu peasant is paying his profoundest adoration to an emaciate Saint. That is to say, there seems to be some organic centre in each race so much more developed than in the other that it may be woken to delirium or frenzy or ecstasy by a spectacle which leaves the other unmoved.

I say some such changes in the organic constitution of humanity were taking place in the

Roman Empire, and that quite independently of the little band of propagandists who called themselves Christians (see Walter Pater's "Marius"). Under Marcus Aurelius a wider sense of *humanity* was growing up. Hospitals, orphan schools, hospitals for animals even, began to be founded. Oriental ideas and religions and (perhaps more important still) Oriental blood and heredity began to circulate. A new type of human being demanded new gods; and men and women whose hearts began to respond to the power of gentleness, the pity of Life, the presence of Death, who, as slaves or the descendants of slaves, knew well what it was to be despised and rejected, began to see a glamour in figures of a different complexion from those which had dominated their predecessors. Thus at length the personality and life of Jesus of Nazareth, or at least the picture of it drawn by Paul and the Evangelists, gave form and outline to this new creative Idea, and it took the shape of the gentle, loving, and crucified Christ, the God that above all has dominated the Christian centuries. Not that this ideal was (as I have said) absolutely new; for the glamour of it, or of something very similar (allowing for difference of race and longitude), had been embodied six centuries before in the figure of the divine Buddha, and doubtless for centuries in the human race these feelings had been registered in race-memory and had struggled for expression; but new as a recognised ideal this undoubtedly was in the history of the Western world.

And (what I wish to enforce) this figure of Christ—written about, pictured in canvas or in stone, or in words of living eloquence, through all these later centuries—has served to waken in the human mind the consciousness of a very real Presence: a Presence at least as real as that indicated by Apollo or Athené to a Homeric Greek: a definite individualised Power which has established itself living and moving in the Western races, and therefore also in each man or woman of these races. In this particular case we have the advantage of being able to analyse an actual and still operative conception of a god; and I take it that the intense reality which this figure carries with it to many people means a great deal. It means that the figure not merely represents a mental ideal of desirable qualities, or the remembrance of a certain beneficent man who once lived, but that it represents a living focus of life in the European peoples of the last two thousand years, which has slowly emerged to consciousness through the accumulated race-memories of a far longer period than that. And I take it that the inward Vision of this living power and presence has in some degree come to most people who have been Christians in anything more than name; while to some people it has come with such force and intensity that they have been persuaded that they beheld the veritable Christ himself surrounded with glory (*i.e.* seen in the luminous field of a superior consciousness). At any rate to deny or utterly discredit all the stories of the Saints, from St. Paul who saw a great light and heard a voice, onward through endless cases to modern times, would be, as I have already suggested, a parochial and purblind view to take.

In the same way I think it seems very unscientific to regard the common stories of 'conversion' as mere fancies or fabrications. It is pretty clear that they represent a reality, a very real experience, to those concerned; and though the 'conversions' may not be as luminous or profound as that of St. Paul, it seems to me that they are things of the same kind—cases, namely, in which after long and silent preparation, new centres of life are suddenly disclosed within folk, accompanied by more or less of excitement, vision, and a complete change of outlook on the world. And the stories, often fantastical enough, which accompany such conversions, must be looked on simply as the lame effort of uncultured minds to picture and interpret the cosmic facts experienced. (See two interesting chapters on "Conversion" in Professor William James' book on "The Varieties of Religious Experience," in which he views conversion as a possible shifting of centres of consciousness, or as possibly comparable to the changes of equilibrium in a polyhedron, resting on one facet after another.)

On the other hand, if we regard the Vision of Christ—as it comes to many people even nowadays—as indicating a real power and presence living and working within them, so we must of course regard the Vision of Athené, or Apollo, or of any other god that came to men and women of old, as indicating a very real and living power within *them.* These are names which Humanity through the ages has given to its own powers and faculties; and every individual, as far as he has truly revered and identified himself with the God that moved within him, has so far identified himself with the life of Humanity.

If we were to go to India, we should find this appearance and presence of the gods everywhere acknowledged and believed in. The vision of Siva, or Vishnu, or Brahma, or of Kali, or Krishna, or any one of the many popular saints who, having once been men, are now become divinities, is common enough. I may give one instance, which will help to remove the matter from the region of mere vulgar fantasy and superstition. Among the Gñánis and Teachers (gurus) who carry on the tradition of the ancient Wisdom-religion from very remote times, and some of whom are among the most emancipated, keen-minded, and inspired of human beings, it is said that a pupil (chela), after all instruction by the Guru, may spend a long time before his initiation is quite complete; then, in the ripeness of time and of his growth, one day (or night) the God (Siva), awful and glorious in light, will appear to him *clothed in the form of his Guru;* and the chela, overcome with amazement and emotion, will leap up, and seeking out his

Teacher will throw himself, in a flood of tears and of gratitude, at his feet. After which his initiation is fulfilled, and he is received into the long line of those who are followers of the god.

Cases of this kind I have personally heard of. (The reader also will remember the quotation from Dr. Bucke in chapter viii.) And there is no reason, I think, to doubt that the above is at least a fair account of what usually happens in the Indian initiations. If so, it illustrates remarkably what has been said all through—namely, that when the Vision in the supernal consciousness, with its accompanying blaze of splendour, takes place, it clothes itself generally in the shape of some figure which is known to the ordinary consciousness, and which is, as it were, the best representation it can get for the purposes of the latter consciousness.

There are other figures connected with Christianity on which I can only dwell briefly. The rise of the Virgin Mary or Madonna into a goddess (with her special services and Temples), is a mark of change similar to the rise of Christ himself—though perhaps not so pronounced. The Madonna links on very closely to Isis, Demeter, Ceres—the ever-virgin, yet ever-fertile goddesses of the elder world; yet her motherhood has more of *human* feeling in it and less of Nature-symbolism than theirs; and her worship marks perhaps a growth in Humanity of filial worship and respect for Woman. When one thinks for a moment of *what* the Mother is to every human being, of the profound impression her figure makes upon the child, and then considers how long, what numberless times, in the history of mankind and in the heredity of every individual, that impression has been repeated on the sensitive film of consciousness; then one sees it as inevitable that there *must* come a time when the Mother-figure should be deified, and become surrounded with this halo of race-memory—that a Mother-god should arise, corresponding to the Father-god of patriarchal times. (Indeed there is much evidence to show that the Mother-god is the more primitive of the two.) As to the Virgin-Mother of Christianity, it is said that St. Bernard of Clairvaux (1100) was much devoted to her. "His health was extremely feeble: and once when he was employed in writing his homilies, and was so ill that he could scarcely hold the pen, she graciously appeared to him, and comforted and restored him by her divine presence" (Mrs. Jameson, "Legends of the Monastic Orders," p. 144). And the number of similar records of Visions of the Madonna must run into hundreds, if not thousands. Whatever we think about these records, their mere existence convinces us how deep, how much deeper than just one individual life, the figure of the pure, long-suffering, tender, divine Mother has etched itself into the heart of the race.

But the rise of Woman, and her influence,

brought another result with it—the deification of the Babe. It is not likely that Man—the human male—left to himself would have done this (though it appears that the Fanti on the West Coast of Africa have a curious worship of an Immortal Child). But to woman it was natural. What woman to-day bending over her sleeping infant has not at some time been aware of a Divine Child which seemed to come and blend its features with those she gazed on? The long heredity of Mother-love and memory is there, and it is not only the little thing before her, which she sees, but the long and wondrous dream of the past which its image awakens. This glamour of the Child arising primarily in the woman, transmitted itself, of course, to the man, transmitted itself to the race generally, and becomes symbolised in such figures as the infant Jesus, the child Horus, the holy Bambino at Rome, and so forth—giving perhaps a tenderness and humanity to Christianity which we miss in the earlier religions.

Thus the Holy Family—Father, Mother, and Child—consolidated itself. For indeed the Family (in this close and limited form) was a peculiar characteristic of the Egyptian and of the Christian centuries; and human life, the human organism, was establishing itself round this as one of its important centres. In the earlier and more primitive and communistic phases of society, the tribe, the *gens*, the clan, the *demos*, were the important groups—the family (in the modern sense) was weak. But with the rise of the Property-civilisation and the breakdown of the older Societies, the individual ceased to find his life and well-being in the tribe or community, and took refuge as it were in the lesser Family, which became sacred and all-important to him as the Ark of his better self and affections amid the troubled waters of external strife and competition. Thus the Family gathered sacredness through the cen turies till it became deified in the mediæval eye.

Looking back then at what has been said, we seem to see the gods arising as Humanity's consciousness through the ages of its own life and faculties (called into play, no doubt, through contact with Nature). Each race, representing some aspect of the great World-self, and inspired and moulded from within by the formative Ideas belonging to it, becomes conscious of these creative powers as the Gods. The gods are in that sense real emanations and expressions of the World-self. And again each individual of the race, affiliated to the race and the gods from whence he springs—or at least to whom he owes his body and his heredity—does through that body and that heredity at times enter into the race-consciousness, and become aware of these powers working within him and the race. Each unit-mind is an offshoot of the racial mind; each unit-body an offshoot of the racial body; and as far as, for each individual, his mind and body register the Life and Memory of the Race do they form a gate of access to its particular Olympus and group of divinities.[1]

In this view, Plato's heaven of eternal changeless Forms and Essences might be compared to the great uplifted Consciousness of the Human Race. In the latter, Forms are seen in the inner Light, which certainly to the momentary individual apprehension *seem* eternal, unchangeable—centres of immense life and activity, mountainous in grandeur, though possibly, like the mountains, really in slow flux and change: great gods, who on their inner side are Wisdom and Justice and Beauty and Courage and Mother-Love, and so forth—in essence the same in all races and peoples; but on their outer side, and with respect to the circumstances and conditions of their activity, are very various from race to race. And the mortal figures that we see, and the images and idols of the Temples, acquire much of their sanctity from the fact that they are expressions or manifestations or reminiscences of these. But of idols I shall speak in the next chapter.

[1] But we must not forget here, what I have hinted more than once before, that race-life is not by any means the only higher order of life to which we have access; and that in every individual slumbers even the absolute World-self. But the race-life and consciousness is interesting to us here as forming the key to what we call the Gods and Religion.

X

THE DEVILS AND THE IDOLS

BUT some one will say—If the Gods are thus real powers and centres of vitality in the human body and in humanity at large, what about the Devils? What are they?—The reply of course is, They are the same. The devils are very real powers and centres of human energy and vitality. But yet there is a difference; and the difference may perhaps be broadly defined thus—that the Gods are powers making for Life and Harmony, and the Devils are powers making for Discord and Death.

There are centres in the human body and mind which make for Corruption: we know that. There are centres of Disease in the body, alien growths which consume and waste its substance; centres of Disease in the mind, alien and consuming passions, ungoverned greeds and desires, hatreds, vanities. There are such things as Lust without love, Desire of food and drink without reverence for Health, love of Power without Pity, love of Gain without Charity. Every one sees that here are centres of activity in the human being which in the long-run must lead to Corruption and Disintegration. There are similar centres in society at large and the life of the race. If the higher centres and those which lead to beneficial and harmonious and permanent activities are the foci where the Gods dwell, then these others are the seats of what we call diabolic and demonic agencies.

The personification, the glamour, the domination of the latter are as easy to explain as of the former. Take any one of the instances above—say the Love of Power. Far back in the history of the race, did the domination of one individual by another (little known among the animals) begin. How many thousands and thousands of times to the ancestors of each of us has the face of some petty tyrant made itself hateful? how deeply have his cruelties, his meannesses, seared the memory of his features in the heart of his victim? how intensely may this long line of memories have come down surrounded by a glamour of fear and hatred? how easy to see that a certain similarity of features and expression in this long line may have given rise to the joint picture of a diabolic figure delighting in cruelty and tyranny—a veritable Satan, composite indeed of race-memories, yet lurking terrible in the subconsciousness of every child, and even of the adult man or woman! Or, to take another example, how many thousands of times to our feminine ancestors may the features of Lust without Love have made themselves fearful and terrible? and how easily out of the combined memory of these may the likeness arise of a devil of Lust and Sensuality, haunting certain centres of imagination and association in the brain! And so on.

But there is another side too to the question. Not only do we all bear in our heredity the remembrance of countless tyranny suffered, and the vague image of a devil corresponding, whom we hate; but we also and similarly bear the remembrance of tyranny *inflicted on others*, and the pleasure accompanying (from immemorial time) such exercise of power. Over and over again the lower human and animal nature within our countless ancestors has rejoiced in its sense of power accompanying some cruel and tyrannous action, till at last such actions have been invested with a sort of glamour, and the temptation to tyrannise (actually to inflict pain) may come down to us with an attraction otherwise hard to explain. Or change the wording of the above, and for Tyranny read Selfishness, Greed, Lust, and so forth, and we see that the argument is the same. The Greed that we hate in others with a composite hatred has a fatal and complex hold on ourselves; and the devil-figure whom at one moment we detest, at another moment exercises over us a strange and lurid fascination, pushing us on to the very deeds we abhor.

The strange psychology of passion is difficult to understand in any other way—the inordinate enchantment which surrounds the pleasures of the Senses, so disproportionate to the actual enjoyment experienced; the mania to which it may rise—of Drink, or Greed, or whatever it may be; the sense (so frequent) of a diabolic power impelling one; the abhorrence, even while they are being perpetrated, of the actions which we call our own. All this seems only explicable by the fact that we bear in our bodies the experience and memory of countless beings, who, *having witnessed or embodied the same action from opposite sides*, transmit to us on one side an intense and reduplicated magnetism in its favour, and on the other side a multiplied hatred of it; and from both sides the sense of a sinister Agency at work within. The strife between human beings in the past, and arising out of the life of the senses, is re-enacted, in miniature and in memory, within our own breasts; there the reconciliation waits to be worked out, and the strange Justice of Nature to be fulfilled! But it is obvious that where such conditions exist, and the sense of the diabolic is present, we are dealing with centres which contain the elements of strife and disintegration within themselves, and which are therefore leading towards Corruption, Insanity, and Death.

But it will be asked, If the devils represent centres of corruption, how can they be related or assimilated to the gods, who are the expression and embodiment of great formative Ideas? The answer is, Simply enough, because the devils also represent formative ideas, but ideas of a lower grade, which necessarily in time have to be superseded. These particular centres of activity, in fact, in the human race, and human body, have not always been centres of corruption or degeneration —quite the reverse—though there are various ways in which they may have become so. Originally perfectly natural and healthy (like all the animal instincts, say), and therefore carrying the sense of pleasure and goodness with them, yet any one of them may in course of time become disproportionately developed, and lapse into conflict therefore with the rest of the nature; or it may, as it grows, develop seeds of strife within itself; or, as Humanity grows and changes and adjusts itself round other centres, the centre in question may have to be readjusted or broken up. In any of these cases the sense of evil will be developed in connection with it; and the continuance of the centre in its particular course will involve the threat of corruption and death to the race or the individual. Thus the Agencies or Personalities which are associated with these centres take on a maleficent aspect. They may not have worn this always. They may have been Angels and Gods (and the power and fascination that they exercise is mainly due to the long far-back and beneficent root-activity of the ideas which they represent in the human race); but now they are become falling Angels, dethroned Gods, Lucifers with a lurid light upon them; and the pleasures and activities associated with them have become delusive pleasures, insane and fruitless activities, stricken and made barren by the pain and suffering of others who are involved;

they stand for Motives which are being ejected from the bosom of Humanity.

To this class belong a vast number of material and animal pleasures and satisfactions. What joy remains in the mere acquisition or spending of Wealth when the inevitable suffering of those from whom it is wrung begins to be realised? or what in ambition or domination or selfish gratification when the others who represent the reverse of the shield are considered and cared for? Not that the ideas of Wealth, or Praise, or Power, or Passion, may not in essence be perfectly good and useful, but the special forms which they have hitherto worn have proved unworthy, and are being superseded or modified. The root-ideas are changing their aspect.

It is needless to recall in detail the fact that the gods of one age or race become the devils of another. It falls naturally into place here.

With Christianity, as we have seen, the human mind grouped itself round other centres of interest and activity than in the old paganism. A tremendous revolution, in fact, in humanity was taking place, and the physiological equipoise was tending towards a denial of the more animal and natural centres in favour of the more spiritual and ascetic. The pagan centres of life became decadent, the pagan gods were changed into devils. Apollo became Apollyon; Aphrodite (or Venus), the stately goddess of Love, Queen of the world and rewarder of heroes and warriors, became a mere demon and enchantress; and Pan, that wonderful impersonation of animal Nature, wore his horns and goat's-hooves now in the character of Satan! But similar revolutions had taken place before; and as the gods of Christianity were now driving out the gods of Olympus, so had these in their time driven out Cronos and Rhea and their crew; and these again had disenthroned the primitive deities Uranus and Gaea—strange far-back records of the growing life of the races within whose bosoms these gods dwelt!

The hatred felt by one race for the gods of another and neighboring race is a thing of the same kind. It is almost a physiological hatred; and it indicates the great constitutional gulfs and differences of habit and life which separate the races. Baal and Ashtoreth were very respectable deities among the Phœnicians, and no doubt were at one period the emblems and expressions of their best life; but for the Israelites they were simply devils. I am not sure that the Saints of the Catholic Church are not by some Nonconformist sects looked at in the same light; and it is obvious that the great division of Europe into Catholic and Protestant and Greek Church is not so much a matter of intellectual rightness or wrongness of view, as of a difference of instinctive heredity, and a distinction of race-feeling between Latin and Teuton and Slav. From the same point of view, the way in which the race-gods figure in all race-conflicts, and the immense importance ascribed to them and their prevailment over the enemy, is a matter very easily intelligible.

But to return to our devils. As I have said, the devils are gods which have gone astray—Powers or Forms which, once helpful and constructive in the human organism, have now become maleficent and destructive. Perhaps in the most primitive races it is not always easy to distinguish gods from devils. The instinct of self-preservation, for instance, is one of the earliest and most powerful instincts in animal and human life. It is largely represented in the lowest savages by Fear. Fear rules in this centre of self-preservation. Everything that can possibly harm the man is dreaded and avoided; mental ingenuity is taxed to discover what may be possibly harmful. Fear is thus good, and a necessary condition of animal life and primitive human preservation. But it is also bad and destructive, and the more advanced the creature becomes, the more so. For as soon as the human brain becomes sufficiently developed to be capable of consciously entertaining within itself the images of Fear—*i.e.*, the images of harmful and horrible things—it is already harming and injuring itself. Fear has already become destructive within it. The images of fearful things within the brain are already beginning the work of destruction which the real things in the outer world are accused of.

Thus Fear is one of the most primitive, powerful, and widespread of the emotions; for a long time it rules in the centre of animal and human life; and it has a beneficent as well as a maleficent aspect. From all this it can easily be understood how prolific a source it has been of deities, good and bad; and how among primitive races certain images (invested) with an agelong glamour of ancestral terror become transformed at last into veritable gods or devils. It does not matter whether they are wooden idols of a certain form and feature, or whether they are snakes' skins, or leopards' claws, or whether they are images of lions or crocodiles, or whether they are real lions or crocodiles, or whether they are black stones or hideous personifications of the powers of the air with a hundred eyes and a hundred arms—it does not matter whether it is the most innocent and harmless object, or the most really dangerous, as long as it is *thought* terrible, as long as the transformation of the race-memory invests it. It is sufficient to remember the fowls. When the sweep's brush leaps out of the chimney-top, when the cap flies up in the air, or even when the harmless solitary rook wings across the sky, Dame Partlet does not stop to scrutinise the object in the dry light of her own reason, but in the glamour of her race-memory instantly *sees* the Hawk-devil impending overhead, and flies for her life.

Even among ourselves—civilised though we be—why do certain faces, certain expressions, certain grimaces, especially in childhood (and even if only portrayed on paper) afflict with such a painful and unreasoning sense of horror? Why is the *dark* so much more alarming to children (not to mention adults) than circumstances seem to justify? Why does such a simple thing as having some one walk continuously behind one in the street cause fidgets and creeps intolerable?—except that these things wake memories in us—memories innumerable of being pursued by man or animal, memories of time when the dark *was* full of danger, far more than now; and so forth. Lafcadio Hearn indeed, in his "Exotics and Retrospectives," suggests that the common nightmare in which one seems to lie powerless in the grasp of some terrible creature of uncertain outline arises in this kind of way. How often, he asks, going back through one's countless primitive-human and animal ancestry, has it not really happened that a fore-father or fore-mother has so lain, and been overpowered, by the foe; and this terrible moment and others in like succession, burning themselves in the brain, and transmitted to descendants, have fused into the awful imagery of the dream, in which the very confusedness of the obsessing Figure is suggestive of its multiplex origin?

Thus Fear in the human race has been the source of countless deities, idols, fetishes, which have been invested in their various degrees with supernatural awe, or fascinating dread, or the most unreasoning terror, and which in proportion as Fear itself, with the growth of humanity, has tended to be cast out, have tended also to lapse into devils, charms, and playthings, and to lose their ancient authority. While again in the form of Awe, and especially associated with the marvellous and impressive moments and aspects of the planets and heavenly bodies, the same feeling has been the origin and inspiration of many of the grander and more enduring gods.

But Fear of course is by no means the only primitive emotion which has cast its glamour over objects and builded up deities. Sex, Hunger, the Mother-instinct, and many other passions, have thus projected themselves. The pagan gods of the Senses and Passions—the fact that these deities were honoured as gods and not feared as devils—shows that these instincts were on the whole healthy and in place. In fact one sees with the passions generally that they are healthy as long as 'in place'; and that their unhealthiness and devilry comes in when they usurp power and cease to be properly subordinate. With the incoming of Christianity, as I have already said, many of these deities became distinctly devils—partly perhaps because the passions corresponding *were* losing their natural place and balance at that time, and partly because by the strong Christian reaction towards asceticism a kind of artificial overturn was being given to human nature. One feels that as long as Aphrodite occupied an honoured and gracious position in the Greek Olympus, the passion which she represented must have been mainly honourable and gracious among those who worshipped her When she fell, it became possible for the monkish writers to regard woman as the incarnation of all filth and wickedness. No Goddess of Love exists in modern times, alas! for indeed Love seems to have fled from public life into the utmost privacy and concealment, leaving only Prostitution and the Divorce Court as its visible reminder in the world.

The distinction between gods, devils, idols, fetishes, magical forms, &c., seems to be only one of degree. They are all cases in which an image, by virtue of association or memory, excites in the mind of the individual beholder a state of consciousness belonging to another order than that of his ordinary life; and it is this extended consciousness which fills him with amazement and impresses him so profoundly.

Fetish-worship is common enough, not only among savage peoples, but among modern nations. One of the most striking instances is that of a child with its doll. Think of the passionate love and admiration, the veritable ecstasy, which the little girl feels at the sight of its friz-haired, blue-eyed babe. The latter's waxen nose has long ago been melted away by the fire, and the sawdust has run out of its legs; but that makes no difference. It is still the doll. The child knows perfectly well that the thing is not a baby, and has no sense or feeling, but it makes no difference (any more than it makes a difference to the fowls that they know quite well my cap is not an eagle). It is still the doll—the symbol, the hieroglyph, which wakes in the child's mind the immense ancestral emotion of countless mother-love and passion flowing down like a stream into its young life, and filling it with amazement.

A great deal of ignorant contempt has been showered upon the worship of idols. But this is because the civilised man does not for a moment see or imagine what the idol means to the savage—any more than as a rule he understands what the doll means to his own little daughter. The savage knows as well as the civilised child (if either of them go so far as to analyse their consciousness) that the object of his devotion is a mere stock or stone Yet what is that to him? To him the real and important fact is, that this painted monster (this effigy which for a hundred generations has played its part in the history of his ancestors) overwhelms him with emotion—with Wonder and Fear and the rude smitings of Conscience—and compels him to bow to a Life, a Presence, which he cannot fathom.[1]

Or (to take an instance which appeals to the civilised man), consider for a moment the inordinate magic of Gold. For a vast period gold has been the symbol of power and well-being, and an object of pursuit. The inherited emotion

[1] "There is a great, secret, deep, vast and unspeakable joy in Idol-worship. Other highest experiences also cannot be comparable to this. As the letters, which stand only in sounds, have been formed and are the cause to learn the intellectual powers; so is the idol formed for the formless god—that we may know by experience the vast intellectual being of his existence."—*Extract from a letter received from India.*

of all those generations is in each of us, and flows swiftly, almost whether we will or no, towards the symbol when it appears. This little old woman, half-starved, and in clothes rusty-green and ragged with wear, walking the streets of London, with her thousands in the Bank, and her beady eyes glittering as she fingers the coins in her purse, is only an extreme case. There is something pathetic surely about her figure; for all these privations she suffers, all these sacrifices that she makes, are not really for the little gold pieces. They are only because the gold pieces wake in her such wonderful memories, and the dim consciousness of the great life behind her, filling her with a strange joy she cannot explain. This, indeed, is her religion.

Or the Fetishes of Royalty and Titles. How explain the glamour which is upon these things, and the anxiety of American pork-dealers to take part in them—a glamour which persists even when reason exposes the very prosaic and commonplace characters of those concerned—unless here again a transcendent sentiment is involved, and an instinct built up and confirmed during thousands of years?

A curious case of fetish and magic is that of spells and incantations. A spell is a spell. That is, it is the use of a form of spoken or written words. To-day the use of words has for the most part become commonplace; but there has been a time far back in history when to convey meanings in this way was little short of miraculous. Especially has this been true of the written word. There existed a few years ago, and probably yet exist, tribes in Central and South Africa to whom a piece of written paper —a letter in fact—was *taboo.* They would not touch it or come near it, for the fear and awe the mystery of writing inspired.[1] In all early peoples writing is confined to the few; and to the many, for generation after generation, it is surrounded with such an atmosphere of wonder, that at last it comes to partake of the supernatural. The Bibles and other writings of such peoples largely owe their sacredness to this fact —often more to this than to the value of the matter which they contain. And more than this, it is probable that *actual forms of words* used in such writings—in Bibles, poems, prayers, recitations, incantations—used over and over again for scores of generations—come at last to carry with them a volume of race-memory and race-consciousness so great as to give them a quite different value and force from ordinary language. How much of the magic which surrounds certain collocations of words in poetry is due to this fact —that they recall threads of ancient experience woven, as it were, in our very blood? As to spells and incantations, is it not really possible that certain forms of words, which have been used for immemorial time, *have* the power of waking in us forms of the race-consciousness with which they have been associated—and so under

[1] See chap. ii. p. 26.

their influence Satan or other powers of light and darkness may indeed appear!

The same sort of thing is true of the magic of numbers. If written words excited wonder among the uninitiated, much more would numbers and their properties and signification. After a time they became positively sacred, and even to-day for many people (theosophists and others) a 3 or a 4 or a 5 or a 7 bear some kind of religious glamour about them, and mystic meanings ineffable. The same too of simple geometrical figures, squares, and pentagons and hexagons; and it is not difficult to understand how these and the numbers entered into and became part of charms and incantations.

My object throughout is to make it clear that all these things—these deities, devils, and fetishes, and the excitement produced by what appear commonplace and unimportant symbols—indicate real stirrings within us of another order of life and consciousness than that with which we are usually concerned, and that it is this fact which gives the symbols or images their value and potency. What further meanings this stirring of another order of consciousness within us may have, and how it relates to our individual lives and personalities, we may consider later on. Here it is sufficient to note that it seems to be the explanation of a vast number of phenomena that otherwise are obscure Everywhere this glamour is to be found. How easy to see or feel, as suggested in an earlier chapter—when we look, for instance, at the young moon in the evening sky (in itself, of course, an impressive spectacle)—that it is not merely our individual eyes that are following that luminous crescent over the mountains, but that within us millions of eyes are gazing, with a thrill of multitudinous emotion far beyond the experience of one twilight scene or one life! How easy to see that the sceptre or rod which the King bears in his hand (or Whip on the Egyptian monuments) carries a glamour of awe with it, because the actual rod in times past descended on the backs of our successive ancestors and left an accumulated impression there, still vibrating in heredity!

The various animals which (naturally) played so important a part in the life of the early races, and entered so deeply into their consciousness, became invested with a corresponding glamour; and there is hardly a creature—bird or fish or bull or cat or beaver or kangaroo—which by some race, Egyptian or African or Australian or American Indian, has not been made fetishistic, totemistic, or divine. The same of many trees and plants. As to parts of the body, it seems natural enough that the phallus and the yoni in almost every race of the world have been treated as objects of worship and emblems of devilry or divinity; for these symbols appeal to every human being, and for good or bad the accumulated ancestral magic surrounding them must be enormously powerful. But even other parts of the body partake of the same enchantment, and it is well known that the mistress's eyebrow, or the hair, or the hand, or even some article of clothing, have in cases a kind of supernatural attraction, which we may fairly ascribe to a more specialised subconscious association of the same character.

A curious instance of the rousing of the communal or race consciousness is given by the word *testis*, which signifies both a *witness* and a *testicle*, the double signification being illustrated by the fact that among many peoples the taking of an oath is confirmed by the placing of the hand on the part indicated. More than any other fact this helps us to understand the sacredness of sex in some early times, and how the sense of the communal life and divinity in connection with sex was so strong, that an oath taken thus was as good as taken in the presence of the god.

XI

BEAUTY AND DUTY

In the above lights it may be worth while to say a few words on the subjects of Art and Morality Beauty and Duty are two of the great formative Ideas of which we have spoken. They operate especially in the more advanced sections of the human race; and wherever they make their appearance they modify Life profoundly. Like all the ideas, they are on one side an incommunicable, unanalysable, innate feeling or sense; on the other side they are structural, and built up of many and various elements. The 'sense of Beauty,' the 'sense of Duty,' are each peculiar, unique feelings. They may be little or much developed, little or much manifested; but they come from within, and are as indescribable as the peculiar smell of a flower. On the other hand, they express and manifest themselves externally in endlessly various forms and structures.

If we remember what has been already said about the Race-life, we shall see that the Idea of Beauty, or the Idea of Duty, will take form in the long succession of the generations of the race largely in accordance with the conditions of that life. That is, the one Life, or Being, or Self of the race, impelling its individual members to honour and cherish the race (in each other), or to sacrifice themselves for it, will stamp upon each individual mind a particular *form* or type of Beauty or Duty—which through the repetitions of Heredity will be emphasized and fixed —though such forms or types will differ much from each other in different races, and will depend along what particular external lines the great formative Ideas are able to work in the given cases. Thus the ideals of the various races are formed.

Thomas Hardy, in his very characteristic poem "The Well-beloved," figures a man walking far one morning over hill and dale to visit his bride, and dreaming, as he goes, of her faultless form, "the God-created norm of perfect womankind." And lo! a shape like that he dreams glides softly by his side—so like, that he asks it, "Art thou she?" And the Shape with equivocal voice replies:—

> Thy bride remains within
> Her father's grange and grove."

And he:—

> "Thou speakest rightly," I broke in,
> "Thou art not she I love."

But again the Shape replies:—

> "Nay; tho' thy bride remains inside
> Her father's walls," said she,
> "The one most dear is with thee here,
> For thou dost love but me."

The man is puzzled; but when he reaches the end of his journey, things become clearer; for he finds his mortal bride indeed, but

> "Her look was pinched and thin,
> As if her soul had shrunk and died,
> And left a waste within."

And the mystery is made manifest—namely, that the ideal and the real woman are two very different apparitions:—

> "O fatuous man, this truth infer,
> Brides are not what they seem;
> Thou lovest what thou dreamest her;
> I am thy very dream!"

Here the distinction between the mortal woman and the ideal 'norm of womankind' is made very apparent; and the suggestion is of course made that the former derives her attractiveness merely from the fact of her arousing a reminiscence of the latter.

On the subject of Beauty an immense amount has been written, and Tolstoy in his "What is Art?" though he only deals with writers of the last two centuries, manages to quote some fifty or sixty answers given to the question "What is Beauty?" Whether we agree with his somewhat contemptuous treatment of the philosophers and their divergencies or not, we cannot but be impressed by the fact that such an amazing amount of intellectual activity has been expended on this subject during that period, as indicating indeed its importance.

And here it is interesting to find that Tolstoy groups the fifty or sixty answers of the philosophers under two fundamental conceptions. "The first is, that beauty is something having an independent existence (existing in itself), that it is one of the manifestations of the absolutely Perfect, of the Idea, of the Spirit, of Will, or of God; the other is, that beauty is a kind of pleasure received by us, not having personal advantage for its object."[1] Both classes of definition Tolstoy considers unsatisfactory; the first, because it dwells in a vague and unknown region of mysticism, and is "a fantastic definition, founded on nothing"; the second, because it descends to mere physiology and the senses. But to us surely both are highly interesting. In fact, we see that philosophy only gives two answers to the question; the one is practically that of Plato, the other is that of modern science. The one places the sentiment of Beauty in the perception of an absolute existence in the Heavens; the other, in the reception of a pleasure not having personal advantage for its object—that is, in a pleasure inspired or generated by something beyond the personal life. Both therefore agree in considering the sentiment of Beauty to be derived from our continuity with an order of existence beyond what we usually call our own. In the view of Plato, the dream-figure which walked by the man's side was a reminiscence of

[1] Tolstoy's "What is Art?" trans. by Aylmer Maude, chap. iv.

some celestial Form seen long ago, but still dwelling there, far in the heavens; in the view of Heredity, it was the re-viviscence within the mind, of a luminous form, the complex product or manifested presence of ages of race-consciousness and memory. In either case it was the waking of another order of consciousness within the man.

I shall now (even though the evidence may not seem absolutely conclusive) assume that this general aspect of the question is the right one, and proceed to inquire what we may infer from it.

In the first place, it would seem that if the dream-figure walking beside the man is merely the rehabilitation of some memory within him, its connection with the living mortal woman to whose feet he is making his pilgrimage is of the slightest; and that in that view Love is indeed a sad illusion, as Thomas Hardy, in his pessimistic way, seems to suggest. The dream-figure, which is the real inspiration of the man's love and devotion, is a merely subjective fancy; and the mortal woman only the painful actuality which by some accident chanced to recall a dream.

But it will easily be seen that the whole point of my endeavour hitherto on this subject will have been missed if the kind of vision with which we are dealing be thus characterised as merely subjective. Taking the Heredity view, we cannot refuse to see that the race-life which builds up and projects these Visions, dreams, and glamours is intensely real, and that the visions, &c.,

are quite real and necessary manifestations of it. This race-life is, as a matter of fact, within each of us, and forms the chief, though a sub-conscious, part of our individual selves; we, as conscious individuals, are simply the limbs and prolongations of it. When, therefore, Thomas Hardy's pilgrim sees the "god-created norm of womankind" walking beside him he sees something which, in a sense, is *more* real than the figures in the street, for he sees something that has lived and moved for hundreds of years in the heart of the race; something which has been one of the great formative influences of his own life, and which has done as much to create those very figures in the street as qualities in the circulation of the blood may do to form a finger or other limb. He comes into touch with a very real Presence or Power—one of those organic centres of growth in the life of humanity, of which we have spoken—and feels this larger life within himself, subjective, if you like, and yet intensely objective.

And more. For is it not also evident that the woman, the mortal woman who excites the Vision, *has* some closest relation to it, and is indeed far more than a mere mask or empty formula which reminds him of it? For she indeed has within her, just as much as the man has, deep sub-conscious Powers working; and the ideal which has dawned so entrancingly on the man is in all probability closely related to that which has been working most powerfully in the heredity of the woman, and which has most contributed to mould *her* form and outline. No wonder, then, that her form should remind him of it. Indeed, when he looks into her eyes (for all that she be "pinched and thin"), he sees *through* to a far deeper life even than she herself may be aware of, and yet which is truly hers—a life perennial and wonderful. The more than mortal in him beholds the more than mortal in her; and the gods descend to meet.

That there are many 'norms' and ideals moving and working within the man, within the woman, and within the race, goes without saying; and these, as we have said farther back, are continually growing from age to age, accreting, advancing, and branching in the various sections, branches, families, individuals even, of the race. The gods are no changeless, inviolate beings, but (at any rate as far as their manifestation is concerned) may be thought of as continually growing, evolving; as Robert Buchanan says:—

> "Fed with the blood and tears of living things,
> Nourish'd and strengthen'd by Creation's woes,
> The god unborn, that shall be King of Kings,
> Sown in the darkness, thro' the darkness grows."[1]

Furthermore, it is pretty evident that, as each individual naturally stands more under the influence of one ideal or organic centre than another, and will differ from other individuals in the proportion and arrangement of his centres, so all

[1] "God Evolving." Robert Buchanan.

will fall into groups, so to speak, under their various gods. Thus Plato, in the "Phædrus," explains that Zeus and the various gods move through heaven, each followed by a company of souls, who thus gain a glimpse of the things of the celestial world. And afterwards, when they are fallen to earth, each soul still implicitly belongs "to that particular god of whose choir he was a member," and seeks for his love and mate among such souls. "They then that belong to Zeus seek to have for their beloved one who resembles Zeus in his soul." Similarly the followers of Hera or Apollo, or any other god, "walking in the ways of the god, seek a love who is to be like their god, and when they have found him they themselves imitate their god, and persuade their love to do the same, and bring him into harmony with the form and ways of the god as far as they can."

Thus the man and woman drawn together by great forces deep-lying in the race, reveal to each other their own deep-rooted divinity. And truly when love comes between them there comes for the first time (*pace* Thomas Hardy) something like real knowledge. There comes also a transformation which may be seen—a change and glory which is as real and obvious to the senses as it is far-reaching and miraculous in spiritual significance.

And may we not say (as Schopenhauer says[1]) that it is in this 'Meeting of the Ideas' that

[1] See above, chap. iv. p. 59.

the sense of Beauty, that the Art sense everywhere consists? When an Idea that is struggling for expression within us meets with and recognises the same Idea (itself indeed) expressed again in some outer form—be it man or woman, or flower, or slumbering ocean—there is an infinite sense of relief, of recognition, of rest, of *unity*; we are delivered from our little selves, our little desires and unrest; and with the eyes of the gods we see the gods.

And I take it that it is much the same with the sense of Duty. Much has been written about the Categoric imperative and the Stern Daughter of the voice of God. It is sufficient to see that such expressions point towards a transcendent consciousness, without feeling it necessary to accept all they imply. The sense of Duty derives primarily and essentially from the sense (and the fact) of oneness between ourselves and our fellows. Structurally and through the centuries it may grow and be built up in forms of laws and customs and out of lower motives of Fear and Conformity; but ultimately and in all these forms it is the Common Life asserting itself, and the sense of the Common Life and unity. George Santayana in his very suggestive book on "The Sense of Beauty"[1] points out that Fear, involving subconsciousness of terrors, death, disease, &c., lies behind Duty; while Love, involving subconsciousness of health, vitality and all pleasurable things, lies behind Beauty. And so we may

[1] "The Sense of Beauty." Scribner, 1901, pp. 24, 25.

see that the earlier consciousness of the race, wherein Fear and the unfriendly gods play so important a part, gives birth to the sentiment of Duty; while the later consciousness endues the Beauty form. In Wordsworth we may discern the transition taking place· "Flowers laugh before thee on their beds, and fragrance in thy footing treads"; and among the Greeks already moral actions had become beautiful, and were accounted desirable *because* they were beautiful.

In the end it is the sense of Oneness, and of the One Life, which underlies these two, and perhaps many other enthusiasms; and may we not think that both Duty and Beauty, the sense of Morality and the sense of Art, when they at last realise their own meaning, are taken up and surrender themselves in an Idea of an even higher order, namely that of Love?

That this sense of the One Life—of the race, or of humanity—is not a mere figment, but a very living reality, many folk's experience will testify. Sometimes, under deep emotion rousing the whole being, there comes a glimmering yet distinct consciousness of this agelong existence. Of such a mood Walt Whitman's poems show many examples, but none perhaps more striking than those first lines of "Children of Adam":—

"To the garden, the world anew ascending . . .
Curious here behold my resurrection after slumber,
The revolving cycles in their wide sweep having brought me again,

Amorous, mature, all beautiful to me, all wondrous,
My limbs, and the quivering fire which ever plays through
them, for reasons, most wondrous,
Existing I peer and penetrate still,
Content with the present, content with the past,
By my side or back of me Eve following,
Or in front, and I following her just the same."

The existence of various orders of consciousness is a conception which is becoming familiar to-day. What with the subliminal consciousness of F. W. Myers and the psychical researchers, the subconscious mind of the hypnotists, the race-memory and heredity of the biologists, the cosmic consciousness of some late writers, the ecstasy of the Christian Mystics, and the *samadhi* of the Indian gñanis, we have abundant evidence of a yet unexplored world within us. And some have sought to show that there is a complete gradation onwards from the mere consciousness of the animals through the self-consciousness of the human being, to family, tribal, and race consciousness, and so upward to the cosmic life and Nirvana.

The important thing, I think, at present—without attempting to go into any detail on the subject or to classify what is yet unknown—is to see that undoubtedly various orders of consciousness do exist, *actually embedded within us*; and that the words I and Thou do not merely cover our bodily forms and the outlines of our minds as we habitually represent them to ourselves, but cover also immense tracts of intelligence and activity lying behind these and only on occasions coming into consciousness. Yet these tracts belong to us, and are ourselves quite as much as, and perhaps more intimately than, those commonly recognised. It is the waking of these tracts, and their inrush upon the field of ordinary consciousness, which is held to explain so many phenomena of our psychic and religious experience. To command these tracts in such a way as to be able to enter in and make use of them at will, and to bring them into permanent relation with the conscious ego, will I think be the method of advance, and the means by which all these questions of the perduration and reincarnation of the ego, and of its real relation with other egos, will at length be solved. If we could by any means explore and realise what is meant by that letter 'I'; if we could travel inward with firm tread to its remotest depth, and find the regions where it touches close, so close, on the other forms of the same letter; if we could stand assured, and look around us, in that central land where it ceases to convey the sense of difference and only indicates unity; and if then with lightning swiftness we could pass to the extreme peri phery where in its particular and invincible shape it almost rejoices to stand alone antagonising the rest of the universe; why, then, surely all would be clear to us, and Gladness and Beauty would be our perpetual attendants. It is through the deepening of consciousness that these results will gradually be obtained; and the forms of the race-consciousness are perhaps intermediary stages on the way.

For, as we have seen, it is in the constitution of things that the large and harmonious should prevail over the petty and discordant, and there is a kind of necessity driving us in the happier direction. In memory and experience the overlaying of images tends to the mutual obliteration of defects and excrescences, and the production of a composite and ideal finer than any single specimen. And just as in the case of musical sounds transmitted a long distance through the air, the discords cancel each other, leaving harmony in the end—so in hereditary transmission the elements which are mutually harmonious prevail. The organic centres in the race (or in the individual) which tend to Strength, Peace, Harmony, Life, persist; those which tend to unbalance, pettiness, decay, and mutual conflict, dissolve and disappear. The Angels overcome and eject the Devils. The root-truths, qualities, powers of the Universe move ever forwards to their expression. Beauty, amid the tangle of the superficial and unfinished, shows itself more and more. Man rises from the life of his petty self, to that of his family, his tribe, his race, mankind, finding his greater Self each time in these; and as he does so his gods lose more and more their deformity and terror, and become clothed with harmony and grace.

The primitive gods, the early idealisations, are more local, partial; they represent the mental states of unformed people living in tribes, families, localities. They are grotesque, fearsome, foolish, these Typhons, Mexitlis, Bulls, Grizzlies, Dagons, Satans, and other monsters; yet they linger in all of us still—incarnations of foolish heart-quakings and prejudices, which though dismissed by our better reason still haunt the twilight grounds of our subconsciousness. Farther on and higher in development, we come to such beautiful impersonations as Apollo, Aphrodite, Demeter, Isis, Mary—representing far profounder movements and intuitions of the human mind; or to those general tendencies to deify the King or the Warrior or the Saint, which may be found in most races; and all of these too linger in us, inspiring the great mass of our religion, poetry, ideals, and those enthusiasms which lift us out of daily life into other spheres of emotion and experience. But all these refer to particular aspects of humanity. It is only with the incoming of Democracy in its largest sense that the idealisation of the common Man and Woman, of the human being, irrespective of all adornments, occurs. The Egyptian could see plainly that the mighty Pharaoh, as he drove by in his chariot, was a god, but he could not see that the negro slave, who flicked the flies from his royal master, was equally divine; but Whitman boldly says of the men and women of the street, "What gods can exceed these that clasp me by the hand?" For him the sight of a simple human being was sufficient to wake the glow and the halo of divinity. This latest and greatest idealisation proceeds clearly from the fact that the image or object in such case rouses the glorified consciousness—not of any one line of experience and memory, not of any particular aspect or section of the race, but of humanity itself. When the consciousness in a man has deepened so far that it is in touch with that of humanity, then clearly any human being may wake that deeper consciousness. And its awakening is accompanied by a sense of glory, wonderment, and perennial splendour as great or perhaps greater than that which accompanied the visions of the elder gods.

Here in this perennial, immeasurable consciousness sleeping within us we come again to our Celestial City, our Home from which as individuals we proceed, but from which we are never really separated. It is surely some intimation and sense of this, some need of its revelation, which gives for us the charm of Utopias and dreams of Paradise and Cities of the Sun. What exactly our relation as individuals to that whole and to each other, and what our relation to the past and future, may be, are questions which for the present we need not trouble ourselves with. When it is realised that the central life *is*, and lives and moves, within us, that it is in some sense ourselves, these questions will largely fall away. Every man feels doubtless that his little mortal life is very inadequate, and that to express and give utterance to all that is in him he would need many lives, many bodies. Even what we have been able to say here shows that the deeper self of him—that which is the source of all his joy and inspiration—has had the experience of many lives, many bodies, and will have.

XII

CREATION

We have suggested (Chapters I. and II.) evolution out of the Mind-stuff, through Feeling and Thought, as the essential process of Creation. The primal undifferentiated Being takes form. The movement out of itself is e-motion, feeling; the form into which it moves is thought. The material world, the world of Creation, *is* (as physical science suggests) movement under various forms.

Let us consider it more closely. The protozoic cell moves towards food. There is motion, which we may, if we like, associate with chemical action (chemotaxis); but we cannot refuse also to see that there is a simultaneous e-motion, or desire for food, in the cell-consciousness. The repetition of this movement towards food evolves at last a dim perception of relationship, a *thought* of the object as food; and with this thought of relation, and the repeated action which the object thus excites, comes structure—as of the evolution of tentacles, or swimming apparatus, by which the food may be pursued or seized.

Later on in evolution, objects are conceived not only as food, but as Fear or Anger or Jealousy, or what not. Objects, of course, *are* not fear or anger, but they *wake* these qualities and feelings, and so build the body and the life of the being concerned. They call forth the new births within the soul which determine its manifestation in the world. Fear oft repeated calls forth the long ears of the rabbit or the donkey, or gives to the monkey its structure for climbing trees.

Later again the Me-sense is called forth and descends into operation within man. It too desires food (the applause of others), and so leads to modifications of structure, to adaptations of morals and manners, such as will secure the approval of fellow-beings.

Looking at things in this way we seem to see how, through ages on the Earth, not only the great needs and emotions have given rise to whole races and tribes of plants and animals, but the detailed forms of these have been *thought out* through processes most closely resembling our own human thinking. If for a moment one considers the working of the latter—how if one wishes to solve any question the image-making faculty within supplies a host of chance-suggestions, one of which at last is found to be the form required; or if we consider how the human race at large has worked out any great problem—say that of ship-building—how through centuries and thousands of years tiny suggestions and modifications have been thrown out by innumerable thinkers—most of which have failed and been discarded in the struggle, but some of which have succeeded and been adopted—and how at last the form of a modern ship has emerged: we see at once that the process by which through the centuries the forms of a stag or a walnut tree have been produced are quite similar. They have been thought out. The image-making faculty in each generation of deer or tree has thrown out (chiefly in the seed[1]) casual variations, suggestions, most of which have failed, but some have been adopted. Each individual tree or animal has contributed its tiny share of thought and ingenuity to the success or failure of its own life, and so of the form which it represents. In the vast succession of individuals, of generations, the total mass of accumulated thought and ingenuity has built itself and *embodied itself* in the marvellous beauty, expressiveness, and meaning, of the stag or the tree. These forms, and the forms of man himself, and of the different races of man, are "the result of the selection and chiselling of thousands of minds through the centuries." And, at once, when we realise this view of Nature and Creation, we realise our part in it, our continuity with it all, and the *power*, hitherto undreamed of, which we may wield, if we only seize the whole process in ourselves, and at its very source.

Here then, at this point, comes a change of conception. All down the race-life before us this process of Creation, through intermediary Feeling and Thought, has been going on—on

[1] See p. 30, *supra*.

a vast scale, and over our heads as it were. We have been like puppets in the game; and all these wonderful race-things, these swift powers, these weaknesses and disabilities, which we inherit in our bodies, we have looked upon as fatal in their domination over us—not to be escaped from, not to be resisted.

But now comes a new conception. This Ego which all down the ages has come building up and slowly perfecting the expression of itself, is 'there' still. We are that Ego. It is not an alien tyrant dominating us, it is our very self. It is not somewhere back in the dark infinite. It is here. And with this recognition all life is changed.

The whole life of the Race from which we have come, the whole route, the whole series of thought-processes by which we have descended, is (it cannot be too often repeated) within us, in our bodies, in our subconscious selves. It is not that we have to go rambling afar through great æons of uncertain history and biology to find this Race-life. It—or that branch of it to which we belong—is here and now in our bodies. The memories, the accumulated experiences, habits, the whole thought-concatenation which has built them up, is there—only waiting to be brought again into consciousness. Every one of these organs, the eye, the liver, the thyroid gland, or what not, has been built up for a special use by intensely conscious selective thought. It is, in fact, at this moment a *habit of thought*—having of course, like every thought-structure, a definite form—and capable of being taken up into consciousness again.

The whole life which has been thought out and expressed in the Race before us is in our bodies; *and something more, i.e.* that which has not as yet got itself expressed. The primal being, in which all thoughts of necessity inhere, which underlies all thoughts, and contains myriads yet unexpressed, is in us. It is there, and accessible to our consciousness. When we reach to it we reach the source of all Power.

We are in the habit of regarding our bodies as *material* legacies from the past—that is, as things unintelligent and therefore essentially unintelligible—and accept them, as I have said, as a kind of lumbering fate or destiny, which we may struggle against indeed, but to which we must eventually succumb. But let us look at them as *mental* legacies—as congeries of customs, habits, views, prejudices, thought-forms, handed down, and immediately the whole aspect of the life-problem is changed. The thought-habits thus crystallised in us may not be the best we can imagine; they may be inchoate forms of the race-life, destined to be replaced by superior forms; new needs, emotions, surging within us may find our present outlines inadequate. But the point is that our bodies now will no longer appear as alien and separate things from our minds, but as our own race-mind made visible, and as essentially continuous with and undivided from that which we more specially call ourselves.

And instantly it becomes clear that our bodies, instead of oppressing like a nightmare, may become our most willing servants, and may even be capable of the most extraordinary and unexpected transformations.

For consider for a moment the thought-nature of the mind—that which we *call* specially mental in ourselves. A man's conscious mind (we know it only too well) is a mass of habitual thoughts, prejudices, ways of looking at things. It has often a most rigid outline. He is a hard-and-fast Tory, or a Plymouth brother, or a screaming Radical, or an obdurate Secularist. The form of the mind is distinct and *set;* one can almost *feel* its shape, as if it were a body; indeed one can detect its shape in the curves and lines of the body itself. And this mental form in such cases is so set, that it offers the greatest resistance to the entry of a new thought. You talk in vain to a person of such type; you adduce arguments, instances; you press new facts upon him; but these things roll off again and effect no lodgment Yet at last, when as it were by a surgical operation, a new idea is really introduced into his mind, how astonishing the change! How often a single suggestion or hint from nature or history, finding its way at last into the brain of some Biblical Calvinist, has brought the whole structure of his religion or superstition to the ground, and turned him into an implacable 'freethinker.' In such cases the power of a single idea (germinal as every idea is with a certain life of its own) is something almost terrible. The old thought-structure gives way before it; devastation spreads through the unseen chambers; the man thinks he is going mad, or really loses his reason for a time. Then he emerges—his faculties and activities keyed upon a new conception of life, his mental outlook and habit altered, his body even notably changed. Or the 'freethinker' in his turn, and by exactly similar process, is transformed into a Spiritualist—and the change is written on his face!

This power, this vitality, of a single thought or conception, and its capacity of growth or multiplication from itself like a living organism, are things which I think have not been sufficiently appreciated. It is not only that one hitherto unconsidered thought (or fact) may destroy a whole system of philosophy or of science—may act like a poison on such system unless it can be properly assimilated and digested—but that a similar thought may multiply in the brain of a man and transform his whole existence.

Here is a plain man who has led a workaday life for some years, honest and decent and respected by his neighbours. One day a chance speculation (perhaps in the markets, perhaps on the turf) unexpectedly successful sets him thinking. The idea that he can *make Money*, can get Rich, effects a lodgment in his mind. A kind of fever ensues. The one idea spawns, generates, and multiplies itself. In a few weeks or months the man is deep in all manner of plans, schemes, and speculations, in a few years he is a millionaire, and a pest to himself and society. He is altered in mind and deeply altered in physique and bodily habit. This one idea of Money-making, very old in the Race-experience, and generating and propagating itself down the centuries, has still enormous vitality; and fastening itself to-day upon thousands of brains, and there spawning, completely mono polises and subverts them, reducing them to a kind of slavery—even as it might be some fell disease.

And seriously the question may be asked, Whether the microbial organisms which our scientific instruments reveal to us are not indeed the external forms of beings which seen from within would appear to us as simple or rudimentary states of mind: whether each microbe which constitutes or is associated with a disease is not representative of some attitude of mind (like Fear or Worry) inimical and baneful to the human organism, while those microbes which are associated with health are representative of constructive and harmonious mental attitudes. The planet on which we live swarms with highly complex organisms, which we call human bodies; and we are so constituted that we cannot help crediting each such body with an internal aspect, or mentality, which we call its mind, also highly complex. As we range down through the animal kingdom we can hardly help doing the same thing, and crediting each simpler organism with a correspondingly less complex state of mind. When, therefore, we reach the simplest forms, like bacilli, whose whole life-action consists in one or two very simple operations, including perpetual self-propagation, is it not natural to suppose that each such organism indicates a state of mind of a very simple or rudimentary type—a single organic thought or desire, as we might call it, incessantly concerned in a certain form of action, and in the repetition and reproduction of itself?

Shall we actually discover, ere long, the bacillus of Fear, or of Money-greed, or of Vanity, or of Ambition. It does not seem so very improbable. Why are certain bodily diseases associated with certain mental temperaments? What are those thoughts that are in the air, like microbes—some beneficial, some baneful? What are those microbes which swarm from one brain to another, like thoughts? Professor Elie Metchnikoff in his last book, "The Nature of Man," says that there is a class of tiny organism, he calls *macrophags*, which in old age gnaw and eat away the brain and other organs. What does Worry do? Is it a macrophag?

But leaving this question of the special interpretation we are to give to microbes, let us return to the general fact that our bodies are the legacies of the immemorial thought of our ancestors, that they are those thought-forms, habits, prejudices, consolidated into definite shape and function; then does it not seem clear what a power a new feeling or thought may have and may exercise in disturbing or readjusting the organisation of the body? That 'conversions' and other such experiences change folk in the most amazing way is a fact we have already alluded to. Such things not only shatter and rebuild people's minds, but also their bodies—simply, it would appear, *because* the body is also a system of habits and thought-forms, like the mind—and a system lying in close relationship (in fact, really continuous) with what we call the mind. And does it not seem clear that in cases new thoughts may enter and disturb or modify the body directly, without passing through or delaying in the mind—or at any rate without disturbing it—perhaps because the mind has already assimilated or is familiar with them? I know of cases in which the receipt of so-called bad news, while leaving the mind quite untroubled and serene, has caused a complete prostration of the body for some days; and every one knows of the wonderfully heartening effect on the body of a piece of good news, even at times when the conscious man has forgotten the intelligence, or is not paying special heed to it. No doctor is unaware of the importance of instilling courage and faith into his patient. This attitude of mind apparently spreads through the body, confirming and strengthening its organic processes. Doubt and despair are equally disorganising. A cruel word, wounding the heart, may paralyse all strength in the limbs. One little thought or feeling, and the whole body-structure deranged!

But, naturally, those parts of the body, or consolidated racial mind, which are most recent and nearest to the conscious mind, are most easily affected by new thought. The more complex nerve-centres, the more recently formed plexuses, representing and embodying more highly wrought thought and emotion, are more easily modified, more easily perhaps upset, than the more primitive and simple. In insanity, it is the higher thought-forms and later developed bodily faculties —the moral nature, the extended co-ordination of the limbs—which first give way. In drunkenness the same The man plumps down on all fours, because the 'leg-centre' (at the top of the brain) was in his long history one of the latest formed—and here the thought-habit of uprightness dwells. In hypnotic suggestion a single notion introduced may strangely transmute a man's actions, physiognomy, or even senses of taste or smell. It may act poisonously or curatively on his body.

Still, in all these cases we do not expect to find the fundamental outlines of the body changed —the bones, the muscles, the forms and functions of the organs—or if so, we only expect the alteration to be very slow and gradual. And this —even though we admit the body's close affinity in itself to thought and to the mind—is perfectly natural and rational. For the physical structure of the body, muscles and organs, is immensely old, and represents thought-habits which have been allowed and confirmed and verified by countless generations; and it is not likely they are going to give way at once to some upstart new idea, any more than a blooming old Tory is likely to have his political faith upset by the first young Radical shaver who comes along. Nevertheless the bones and muscles and solider parts of the body *are* altered by thought. Sandow has shown us that. He has particularly insisted on the great influence which concentration of the mind exercises on the growth of the muscles.

Every one must have noticed how certain attitudes of mind are associated with certain attitudes of body—courage and faith with an erect carriage, depression and doubt with bent back and uncertain gait, and so forth. It is clear that when certain attitudes of mind become permanent and habitual, they must permanently alter the carriage and structure of the body. Again, that the chemical nature of the secretions from the various glands and organs is altered in connection with the various emotions—joy, fear, grief, pain, love, and so forth—is a well-known fact; and it is obvious that when these states of mind persist, permanent alterations of the functions of the organs must follow.

Thus we arrive—and the human race is arriving—at the conscious use of the formative power. We are arriving at one of the most fruitful and important turning-points in the history of the race. The Self is entering into relation with the Body. For, that the individual should conceive and know himself, not as a toy and chance-product of his own bodily heredity, but as identified and continuous with the Eternal Self of which his body is a manifestation, is indeed to begin a new life and to enter a hitherto undreamed world of possibilities.

It begins to dawn on us that, identifying ourselves with this immortal self, we also can take part consciously in the everlasting act of Creation. To still the brain, and feel, feel, feel our identity with that deepest being within us is the first thing. There in that union, in that identity, all the sins and errors of the actual world are done away. We are most truly ourselves; we go back to the root from which all that may really express us must inevitably spring.

Remaining there in silence as long as may be, then out of that state will inevitably spring a wave of conscious Feeling—of joy, courage, love, expansion, or whatever it may be—a feeling not foreign or fabricated or ephemeral, but deeply rooted and expressive of our real life. Then holding on to that root-idea, that feeling, that emotion, that desire, whatever it may be, confident in its organic rightness and constructive power—holding steadily to it for a time—perfectly naturally and inevitably out of it will flow certain forms of Thought. The feeling will take shape, it will clothe itself in images of things actual; and already the process will have begun by which those things will be created or realised in the world. "All consciousness is motor," says William James; and no sooner does the new emotion or desire come within the border of consciousness than it sets the springs of action in motion which inevitably flow down to Creation and the outer world.

It is not that any violent act of Will is required for the realisation of things in this outer world. It is rather that by non-acting we should identify ourselves with the great process of Creation for ever going on.[1] There is Will certainly, there is control and power in holding and concentrating on any given feeling or thought; but it is not the violent will which would seek to wrest materials from their places. The driver of a locomotive does not jump down and seek forcibly to turn the wheels of his engine; but moving one or two levers, he controls the great driving forces at their source. So handling the levers of Feeling and Thought we can already send the forces of Nature in our bodies and elsewhere along the lines which we desire.

Long and persevering must the practice and exercise be, by which power to direct thought and feeling may be attained, and by which the sense of identity with the universal self may

[1] "By non-action," says Lao-Tzu, "there is nothing that may not be done. One might undertake the government of the world without ever taking any trouble—and as for all those who take trouble, they are not competent to the government of the world."

be established—for without this latter all our work must inevitably turn out vain and ephemeral—but when the conditions are fulfilled, then strangely obvious is the result and simple the act of Creation.

XIII

TRANSFORMATION

TRANSFORMATIONS are perpetually going on throughout the animal kingdom, and throughout our individual lives.

New ideals, new qualities, new feelings and envisagements of the outer world, are perpetually descending from within, both in man and the animals; new centres and plexuses are forming among the nerves; new gods are presiding in the region of our dreams. Every one of these things means a new centre of life and activity, and a transformation (slow or swift) in the type of the individual or the race.

The transformations induced even by momentary excitement of particular feelings or centres are most extraordinary. See a man under the influence of violent Anger or of Jealousy—his whole mien, face, attitude, exhalation of character changed—it is hardly credible that he is the same person that we knew before. Or see him under the influence of some strong enthusiasm or generous emotion, doing things he would have been physically incapable of at another time!

Or again, when the poison of drink reaches

and inflames some particular centre in the brain, Philip drunk becomes so utterly different from Philip sober that we can only say he is not 'himself'; or when disease or old age or madness act in a similar way, these alterations and alternations of Personality can only be described as *transformations;* taking place, indeed, according as one centre or another in the brain, one synthesis or another in the mind, may happen to be in the ascendant.

Throughout the whole animal kingdom, but especially among insects, transformations of one kind or another are most abundant and remarkable. There are 'recapitulations' by the embryos and young of mammals of the life-history of their race, with strongly marked breaks and mutations corresponding to the stages of evolution represented; there are the metamorphoses of caterpillars and flies, some including twenty or thirty changes in a single life-time; there are the transformations and alternate generations of annelids and crustacea; and there are strange jumps and quick disguises in the lives of some plants. Even the human being passes through a great number of very distinct stages and phases from the embryo onwards to old age.[1]

But probably the greatest and most important of all transformations in the human and animal kingdoms, is that which takes place when the centre of life in Man is transferred, as indicated in the last chapter, from unconscious activity in

[1] See *infra*, "The Mayfly," p. 230 *et seq.*

the body to the conscious self—that is, when the individual self, reaching union with the universal, becomes consciously and willingly the creator and inspirer of the body. That is indeed a Transfiguration. The individual is no longer under the domination of the body and its heredity, but rising out of this tomb becomes lord and master of the body's powers, and identified with the immortal Self of the world.

This transformation, whilst the greatest and most wonderful, is also of course the most difficult in Man's evolution, for him to effect. It may roughly be said that the whole of the civilisation-period in Man's history is the preparation for it. For though the transformation itself (of the consciousness, from the second order to the third order) may be practically instantaneous, yet the pupal condition, during which the elements of the change are being prepared and set in order, must necessarily be immensely protracted; and it must be remembered too, that when for any individual the transformation of consciousness does occur and the new forces begin to operate, it does not follow at once that the change is permanent, and that there will not be backslidings again to the old centres; or that the change in the inward consciousness can be immediately followed by corresponding change in the whole bodily system. Indeed it seems probable that for the individual the permanent change is hardly possible until such time as large portions of the race round him are sharing in it.

Thus, though this great Transformation may individually have an instantaneous character, yet the period of its preparation and establishment may occupy ages of human history. We may divide the latter into three periods: The first, or animal period, in which the human being follows his body and its instincts unhesitatingly; the second, or intellectual period, in which a half-formed, separate and illusive, self appears; and the third, or period of the Super-man (if we like to call it so) in which the self, being identified with the universal being, becomes the centre of absolute recognition and reliance and repose. The great Transformation is that which takes place at the entrance of the third period; and the second period is the period of its preparation.

This transition from the first to the third stage is obviously a very difficult and precarious one. It covers practically the whole of what we call civilisation. During this period the sense of Me-ness has to descend into consciousness, and to be evolved—the sense of self, but of course at first in a very imperfect and illusive form. The (false) notion of a separate and atomic self, apart and having interests distinct from the rest of the universe, for a long time dominates; and for a long time leads to the most terrible struggles and miseries. There is no real reliance anywhere. The old animal instincts and sanctions having been abandoned, there remains nothing but this illusive phantom ego which gives way direfully the moment any pressure is placed upon it. The fight for this self as against other selves, and the everlasting doubt as to where, in the midst of the general chaos, reliance may be found, lead to huge and despairing efforts of the Brain—as it were to solve a double and impossible problem. And the growth and ascendancy of the self-conscious, analytic, individualising Brain becomes one of the great marks of this period. The Brain and Self-consciousness are the midwives, as it were, of this great birth and transformation—the greatest of all births and transformations—of the soul. They are both of incalculable value and importance to humanity; but in their present form, and as long as the true individuality and the true self is unrealised, they both can only be regarded as distorted, unbeautiful shapes, to be redeemed in the future when the present work is done.

There comes a time however, and at last, when—the real self emerging into consciousness, abysmal, adamantine, founded deep below and beyond all worlds—the Brain ceases from its terrified and insatiate quest. Even the far-inherited and age-long animal instincts, rooted in the great immensity of material Nature, yield in respect of authority or promise of security to this far deeper knowledge of the Nature-self. They either fail and shrivel before it, or becoming identified with it lose their separate and external outline; and the first period joining on and becoming amalgamated to the third, leaves only the tiniest crack or seam between to indicate what was once a huge gulf including thousands of years of human history.[1]

The brain is stilled. It does not cease from its natural and joyful activities. But it ceases from that terrified and joyless quest which was inevitable to it as long as its own existence, its own foundation, its own affiliation to the everlasting Being was in question and in doubt. The Man at last lets Thought go; he glides below it into the quiet feeling, the quiet sense of his own identity with the self of other things—of the universe. He glides past the feeling into the very identity itself, where a glorious all-consciousness leaves no room for separate self-thoughts or emotions. He leans back in silence on that inner being, and bars off for a time every thought, every movement of the mind, every impulse to action, or whatever in the faintest degree may stand between him and That; and so there comes to him a sense of absolute repose, a consciousness of immense and universal power, such as completely

[1] When the consciousness deepens to that of the universal life, and to the point whence as it were the different races have radiated, then the figures of the gods grow dim and lose their outline, the rivalries and mutual recriminations of the various human ideals cease to have the old poignancy and interest; and their place is taken by a profound sense and intense realisation of the unity and common life of all races and creatures; by a strange and novel capacity of understanding and entering into the habits of distant beings or peoples; and by a mysterious sense of power to 'flow down' into these forms and embody therein a portion of the life universal. And with all this come naturally great changes in the institutions and political forms of peoples, and the spreading of the genuine Democracy and Socialism over the earth.

transforms the world for him. All life is changed; he becomes master of his fate; he perceives that all things are hurrying to perform his will; and whatever in that region of inner Life he may condescend to desire, that already is shaping itself to utterance and expression in the outer world around him. "The winds are his messengers over all the world, and flames of fire his servants; . . . and the clouds float over the half-concealed, dappled, and shaded Earth—to fulfil his will, to fulfil his eternal joy."

For the ceaseless endeavour to realise this identity with the great Self, there is no substitute. No teaching, no theorising, no philosophising, no rules of conduct or life will take the place of actual experience. This is the Divine yoga or union, from which really all life, all Creation, proceeds. And for its realisation it is necessary that at times, as already said, all thought, all plans and purposes, should be obliterated from the mind, leaving it free to fall back and touch absolutely to its own source. What is learnt by this actual experience is so much more, and so much more important, than anything that can be learnt by teaching or philosophy, that at any rate *without* it the latter can hardly be accounted of much value.

It may, however, be of some use, as a supple ment to the reader's personal experience, to say a few words more. This true Ego—this Self above and beyond the separate Me—to know it one must, as I say, become identified with it; and that is ultimately the only way of knowing it. Yet it may help us, to be able to see, as a matter of speculation, what its nature may and must be.

The true Self is universal: that is, it is the Self of all beings. But that does not mean that it is *not* individual. On the contrary, as far as it is the self of any one being it must be individual. If it is remembered what was said in the chapter on Affiliation it will be seen that every local or individual self exists only by reason of its being an outgrowth or prolongation or aspect of the universal Self, and that conversely the universal self has no definite expression or existence except in so far as it is individual and local in some degree or other. The true and ultimate Self therefore in each of us is universal and common to all beings, and yet it is also individual and specialised in a certain direction. When the more universal nature of the Self descends and becomes revealed, the consciousness of the individual necessarily takes certain forms corresponding.[1]

One of these is Love and Sympathy. The self, hitherto deeming itself a separate atom, suddenly becomes aware of its inner unity with these other human beings, animals, plants even. It is as if a veil had been drawn aside. A deep understanding, knowledge, flows in. Love takes the place of ignorance and blindness; and to wound another is to wound oneself. It is the great deliverance

[1] See note on the great primal Ideas, chap. vii. p. 121.

from the prison-life of the separate self, and comes to the latter sometimes with the force and swiftness of a revelation.

Another form is Faith, Courage, Confidence. If I have my home in these other bodies as well as my own, if my life is indeed so wide-reaching, so universal, if I *feel* that it is so—what is there to fear, how can I fear? All things are given into my hands. My life checked here may flow on there; innumerable are my weapons, my resources; and rooted down, deep, below all accidents, is my real being.

Or again a strange sense of Extension comes on me—and of presence in distant space and time. Mine is an endless Life, unconquerable, limitless in subtlety and expanse; and strange intimations that it is so come to me even in my tiny earth-cell—intimations of power inexhaustible, of knowledge mysterious and unbounded, and of far presence through all forms and ranges of being.

These are some of the things—*some* of the new modes of consciousness that come—Love, Faith, endless Life and Presence in space and time, endless Power, Knowledge, 'Humanity.' Let them be *felt* first. Do not *think* too much about them. When you have merged your being, if it be but for a moment, in its source, then inevitably on emerging (if union has really been effected) will one or other of these feelings that I have mentioned be found occupying your mind. Do not *think*—or at any rate delay the process of thinking as much as you can—but retain the mind in its state of feeling. Feel, feel, feel, in silence, your touch upon the great inner Life, in these its first Creative forms. Rivet and hold fast these feelings; join them ever on to your central and abiding Self; make them into the great main branches of your Life-tree; and so gradually let them pass outward into the twigs and ramifications of thought, to deal with the actual and the outer. Thus they will pass into structure. These feelings, this Supreme Life which they represent, will pass into expression, and become realised in the structure of the body. They will pass into the life around, and become realised in the structure of Society.

The body so built—when it is built—must clearly be æonian, not mortal in the ordinary sense. The mortal, local, and 'separate' self, with its illusive limitations, can only build a mortal and temporary body. The Race-self truly, being æonian, may build, in the institutions and life of the race, an agelong-enduring body. And as far as this race-self enters into the consciousness of the individual—as it does at times through the great enthusiasms of the race—so far does the individual put on the race-body, and share in its degree of physical immortality. But when, further, into the individual there descends a consciousness profounder, more basic, more enduring, even than that of the Race-self, then inevitably does there begin to be built even for the individual, a body corresponding. This body, in fact, is the expression and grows out of those great creative feelings of which I have just spoken. Through Love it becomes a body built into the lives of others, and positively sharing their organic life and vitality. Since Faith and Courage inspire it, it is well based, firm to stand the shocks of Time and Accident; extending its domain over the elements; incorporating in itself the sea and the wild creatures, and so unafraid of them; surrounding Chance and taking it captive. Its consciousness of immense Extension in time and space indicates its ethereal character; its consciousness of Power indicates its strongly material composition; its consciousness of Knowledge, the penetrating subtle quality of it. And so we forebode, beside and within the very local body which we know best (and which is expressive of our more local selves), another body expressive of our more universal nature—a body built of swift, far-extending ethereal elements, subtle and penetrating, yet powerfully massive and material; closely knit in itself, not easily disturbed or dislocated, enduring for æons; yet sensitive in the highest degree, and twining its nerves and fibres through all Creation—sharing the life of all creatures.

Of that body, woven like Cinderella's robe of the sun and moon, who shall speak? "Lo! the rippling stream, and the stars, and the naked tree-branches deliver themselves up to him. They come close; they are his body; and his spirit is wrapt among them; without thought he hears what they and all things would say."

When on the striving, bewildered consciousness, in the maze of the second stage, suddenly the apparition of that body dawns, no wonder there is a transformation and a transfiguration. "Behold I show you a mystery!" says Paul, "in the twinkling of an eye we shall be changed." And Fra Angelico in his little cell at San Marco saw even the same mystery, and in simple vision pictured it out of his own soul upon the wall—the transfigured Christ, luminous, serene, with arms extending over the world.

This sublime Consciousness of simple Being (with which we began these chapters) *is* there—is in the world and within all creatures—as the supreme cosmic Consciousness always. It can be seen quite plainly in the look in the eyes of the animals—and in primitive healthy folk and children—deep down, unsuspected by the creature itself; and yet there, unmistakable. It is seen by lovers in each other's eyes—the One, absolute and changeless, yet infinitely individuate and intelligent—the Supreme life and being; of which all actual existence and Creation is the descent and partial utterance in the realms of emotion and thought.

APPENDICES

THE MAY-FLY

A STUDY IN TRANSFORMATION[1]

EVERY one knows the May-fly—or at least some member of the tribe, of which there are said to be fifty species in Great Britain alone. The most well-known perhaps is that one which anglers call the Green Drake or the Grey Drake, and the scientific folk call *Ephemera vulgata*—a little fairy with four pearly lace-like wings, and whitey-green body about an inch long, and tail of three long hairs. They appear in numbers on any hot day towards the end of May, or in this neighborhood (Derbyshire) in June, and continue to be seen for two or three weeks; and they love to dance—scores and hundreds together—in the sunshine, whizzing vertically upwards for a few feet, and then letting themselves float luxuriously downward on poised V-shaped wings; then up again; and so on for the few short hours of their life—during which they do nothing but dance, make love, and lay their eggs. They cannot eat, for their mouths do not admit of their taking food! Their numbers are sometimes so great that they look like snowflakes in the air, and the ground and even the water are strewn with their dead or dying bodies.

For they come from the water, from running water;

[1] Reprinted from the *Humane Review*, April 1903.

there is no doubt about that. They are found generally near a stream; and if you go down to the stream you will see them rising as if by magic, from the weeds by the brook side, or even from the clear surface of the water. Look closer, and you will see what appear to be empty husks of them floating in the water, or tangled amid the marginal grasses. But though you feel sure these *are* their husks, yet it is most tantalising, for to put the two together and to see the fly actually emerging from its case is most difficult. You may watch for an hour without success—for the trick is done, the lightning change is made, literally "in the twinkling of an eye."

The larva of the common may-fly is a semi-transparent, brownish, scaly creature, clumsy and sluggish, that crawls about the bottom of running streams or hides itself in small semicircular burrows in the banks. "Bank bait" it is called by the anglers, for it too, as well as the perfect fly, is much beloved by the Trout. It remains in this condition apparently for two years or so, during this period casting its skin several times, and undergoing on each occasion slight transformations in structure. At last the wings develop and "become prominent under the larval skin, and the intestine (so says Swammerdam) is emptied, and the colour of the animal changes in consequence." Then it is ready for its transformation.

One day, when the weather is warm, and in its retreat the insect knows that the right moment has arrived, it creeps from its burrow, swims rapidly up to the surface of the water, and there performs the feat which is so difficult to witness. Swammerdam, in 1675, speaking not of *Ephemera vulgata*, but of an allied form, the *Palingenia longicauda*, says:—

"When the larvæ have left their burrows they make their way with all speed to the surface, and the transformation is effected with such rapidity that even the most attentive observer can make out little, except that the winged fly suddenly darts out from the midst of the water."[1]

And Réaumur, observing in 1738 another allied form, the *Polymitarcys*, says :—

"The rapidity with which they cast the larval skin is truly wonderful. We cannot take our arm from the sleeve of a coat more readily than the Ephemera extricates its abdomen, wings, legs, and its long tail-filaments from their sheaths. During the operation they rest upon objects standing out of the water or upon the water itself. The thorax splits lengthwise, and the rest of the business of extrication is over in a moment."

And of their enormous numbers he says :—

"The exclamations of my gardener, who had gone to the foot of the stairs [by the river Marne, near Paris], attracted my attention. I then saw a sight beyond all expectation. The Ephemeræ filled the air like the snow-flakes in a dense snow-storm. The steps were covered to a depth of two, three, or even four inches. A tract of water five or six feet across was completely hidden, and as the floating insects slowly drifted away, others took their place. Several times I was obliged to retreat to the top of the stairs from the annoyance caused by the Ephemeræ, which dashed in my face, and got into my eyes, mouth, and nose."

Any observer who cares to take the trouble will be able to verify the remarks of Swammerdam and Réaumur as to the rapidity of the May-fly metamorphosis, and the difficulty of observing the actual details. For some seasons in succession I watched, on favorable days, in a certain brook, for the transformation of *Ephemera vulgata*, but always without success. At last, however, I was rewarded. I saw what at first I thought was a mere husk floating down the stream ; but there was a silvery glaze at the thorax end. Immediately that end

[1] See Miall's "Natural History of Aquatic Insects," chap. viii.

opened, a perfect May-fly glided out, head first, stood for a moment on the wave beside its own corpse, stretched its wings, and flew away. The whole operation was so rapid that it was completed even while the stream moved forward about three feet, say, in two seconds. Since that time I have witnessed the change frequently. Sometimes the grub seems to creep and wriggle up the bank side till it gets onto a stone or twig just on the water surface; the glistening air-space appears quite at the front end of the thorax. This or the back of the head itself opens, the skin on the two sides turns over, leaving, as Sir John Lubbock describes,[1] only a small aperture, through which, as from a glove, the insect delivers itself—the legs from the legs, the antennæ from the antennæ, the jaws from the jaws, the eyes from the eyes, and the three tail-filaments (in the case of *E. vulgata*) from the three tail-sheaths. But the jaws now, in the perfect insect, are rudimentary, and useless for eating purposes; and the eyes are compound and many-faceted, instead of flat and smooth as they were in the larva. Only the gills, which were large and branched in the larva, are completely gone; and four wings, completely absent in the original grub, now adorn the perfect insect.

Curiously, it appears that even now—at any rate in the case of the common May-fly—the transformations are not finished. For though it has its mature form and power of flight, yet presently its skin splits once more, a final veil falls from its wings and its whole body, and it emerges—lighter both in colour and in weight than at first (the *Grey* Drake now, whereas in its all-but-perfect state it was the Green Drake)—and joins its companions in the mazy dance, in which the remaining hours of its existence will be mostly passed.

Mostly, but not altogether. The one serious duty of the Ephemera is egg-laying and fertilisation. As we have seen, it does not eat. It is freed from the necessity

[1] "Origin and Metamorphoses of Insects," p. 21.

of collecting and consuming food. It has come to the end of its life as an individual, and its only call is to provide for the race. And this seems to be a reason why so many insects put on wings in their final and reproductive stage—or why their egg-laying is delayed to the winged stage—in order, namely, that they may be able to spread their progeny to a distance from the original location. Especially is this true of water insects, which, with the drying up of streams and ponds at certain seasons, might be in danger of perishing entirely, if the perfect creature were not able, being winged, to fly to distant places where the conditions were more favourable.

Accordingly, our Ephemera takes care to lay its eggs in the water of some stream—either that from which it emerged or some other—where its grub will find itself at home. Réaumur, speaking of Polymitarcys, says that "they skim the surface of the water, and support their bodies upon it by means of the tail-filaments while engaged in egg-laying. The eggs fall at once to the bottom, and soon become scattered, for the jelly in which they are embedded is soluble in water." De Geer, speaking of *E. vulgata*, gives much the same account, and adds, with regard to fertilisation, that the aërial dances of the Ephemeræ are usually composed of males only, but that when, as often happens, a female mixes in the swarm, two or three males pursue her, until one of them succeeds in flying away with her—generally to the top of a wall or summit of a tree.

With fertilisation and egg-laying the duties of the individual terminate. The parent insects perish; and the life-round begins again.

The metamorphoses of insects—of which that of the May-fly, with its very sudden transition from a lethargic subaqueous existence to a giddy dance in the sunshine, is such a striking example—are mostly rather dramatic and impressive. But it is well, in considering the subject, to remember that they are only pronounced instances of an event which is very universal in Nature. Slighter transformations are common, and continually taking place. The larva of the May-fly undergoes several minor changes, as I have already mentioned, before its final liberation into the air. One of the species, *Chloeon dimidiatum*, goes through *twenty-one* moults, according to Sir John Lubbock, while it is preparing for its imaginal form. Caterpillars and other grubs, as is well known, frequently cast their skins and take on slight changes of structure or colour. In the case of worms and insects, as there is no interior skeleton, the skin, horny or otherwise, forms the attachment and support of the muscles and internal organs, and with any change of these latter a new skin has to be formed, and the interval of forming the new skin and casting the old one often necessitates a dormant or pupal stage, which may be brief or prolonged according to circumstances. Crabs and other crustacea similarly cast their shells and go through periods of seclusion, accompanied by changes of structure.

In the case, however, of the vertebrate animals and man there is not the same necessity to change the skin, and the transformations are not so obvious. Yet they are taking place all the time. The human being passes through several very distinct phases as an embryo in the womb; besides these there is a marked change at birth; then another at the coming of the milk teeth, and again at the casting of the same; another at puberty; and again another in age, with the lapse of the sexual functions. Possibly yet others of a slighter character might be distinguished. These that I have mentioned as taking place during the actual life of an individual, and corresponding to the growth and change of teeth, to puberty and to the meno-pause, all imply considerable changes of structure and organisation, and (what is worth noticing) are generally accompanied by periods of lethargy, subversion of the system, and even symptoms of disease, which are suggestive, to say the least, of the pupal stages in insects. So far, then, we seem to see that transformations, more or less pronounced, are a common, and one may perhaps say normal, phenomenon of animate nature.

With regard to Man and the Mammalia, it has been, since the time of Von Baer, an accepted doctrine that the successive changes in the embryo and the young form a kind of epitome of the history of the race to which the individual belongs. It is pointed out that the embryo of man, for instance, at an early stage shows characteristics which assimilate it to the fishes, and, later, characteristics which assimilate it in succession to reptiles, lower Mammals, and higher Mammals; that, again, the lately born infant has some characteristics of the monkey or other arboreal animals, and that the boy has the habits and conformation of the savage; and so on. Some of these stages in the development of the individual may be fairly distinct and well marked; others may glide quite imperceptibly into each other. But, anyhow, the point is that the growth of the individual thus resumes and rehearses in brief the agelong previous life and growth of the race. Now the theory with regard to insects seems to be that here, too, the life of the individual, from the egg onward, through all the changes and transformations of the grub, the larva, the pupa, and the perfect insect, is, in a similar way, a recapitulation of the life-history of its race. In a similar, yet not exactly the same way, as will presently be explained.

But first a word about what race-history means.

For long periods in the life of a race, slow growth and modification of the organs and faculties may take place, and yet the general balance of the organic centres in the normal individual may be little changed; the general type of the race may remain much the same. But then again there will come a period or periods when changes of conditions or the natural course of evolution will occasion rather rapid and complete changes in the balance of the functions, possibly even the growth of quite new organic centres. Then the type of the race will alter very decidedly. When, for instance, the monkey-like animal first took to climbing trees, however slow and continuous its development had been before, now a rapid transformation began to take place. A new centre organising and controlling the prehensile activity quickly developed, and soon assumed a commanding position among the other organic centres; the balance of functions in the race suffered a kind of revolution. So when the precursor of the dog first came under the influence of man, a new formative plexus arose which modified the whole mentality and activity of the animal; or when certain kinds of worms or insects by accident or by necessity took to marshy and watery grounds, and ultimately became aquatic, the same kind of thing happened. Thus race-history, from this point of view, means the gradual growth and redistribution of organic centres in the animal; gradual, that is, as a general rule, but varied by occasional rather rapid changes in the balance of these centres and their functions; and may be looked upon as a combination of slow evolution with, now and then, what may be termed revolution.

If we apply this to the history of any single individual —say, of an individual man from his commencement as a germ, through his life and growth as an embryo, a babe, a child, a boy, and so on to maturity, we seem to see the same thing—slow, continuous evolution, interrupted now and then by rather rapid and considerable transformations, and the grouping of the life round new organic centres. Thus, early in the life of the human embryo (between the fourth and eighth week[1]) the

[1] W. B. Carpenter, "Human Physiology," 8th edition, p. 1011.

arrangement of its blood-vessels, which hitherto has been slowly developing on the type of the fishes and cold-blooded animals, begins to transform itself to the type of the Mammals, and at the moment of birth the first use of the lungs completely changes the actual character of the circulation. In fishes the kidneys do not exist, their function being partly fulfilled by certain other bodies; and this is also the case in the human embryo between the fourth and seventh week; but at the latter date the true kidneys first begin to present themselves, and a readjustment soon takes place with respect to these bodies and their importance in the system. Again, with regard to the Brain, Dr. W. B. Carpenter says that in the sixth week of the human embryo there is a "certain correspondence" between its brain and that of a Fish; in the twelfth week there is a "strong analogy" with that of a Bird.

"Up to the end of the third month, the Cerebral Hemispheres present only the rudiments of *anterior* lobes, and do not pass beyond that grade of development which is permanently characteristic of the Marsupial Mammalia. . During the fourth and part of the fifth months, however, the middle lobes are developed . . . and the posterior lobes, of which there was no previous rudiment, subsequently begin to sprout. . . . In these and other particulars there is a very close correspondence between the progressive stages of development of the Human Cerebrum, and those which we encounter in the ascending series of Mammalia."[1]

Here, all along, then, we may see changes of structure and function, and the alteration of balance in the organic centres, taking place gradually or rapidly in the brief life of the individual, just as on an infinitely more extended time-scale they have taken place in the far-back life of the race from which the individual is descended.

[1] Ibid., p. 1034.

Appendix I

And, digressing for a moment, it is difficult in all this—however unwilling we may be to use terms which we cannot fully justify—not to see something very like *memory*. Memory it may not be in exactly the ordinary sense; but when we consider how like the process is to that which we use when recapitulating mentally the events, say, of our past years—the rapid summarising in thought of what has gone before, the actual reassuming in some degree of the old attitudes and expressions—as of children when thinking of our own childhood, or of boyhood when thinking of our school days—the faint and more general delineation of the distant and the slower and more detailed reconstruction of the nearer past; when we think how near habit and custom are to memory, and how physiological habit is often held to explain our resemblance to our ancestors: I say it is difficult not to see in this recapitulation by the individual of the general outlines of the history of his race, something very like the working of a racial memory transmitted to the individual. The expression may not be really our final word on the subject, but it may be practically the best that we at present have at command. And we seem to see the individual creature, when faced with the problem of its own unfoldment, leaning back on its racial memory, and so repeating the things which it finds there, and which have been done before—just as we all, when faced with the daily problems of life, first of all in any case repeat what our own memory tells us we have done before—and only when that process is finished, or fails to serve us, cast about to try something else.

Now, in the case of insects the theory is, as I have said, that each individual insect "recapitulates" the life of the race from which it is descended, in just the same way as does the young of man or the higher animals, but with this difference, namely, that while the young of man and the higher animals recapitulates all the earlier portion of its life-history in the womb of its mother (as an embryo), the young of the insect recapitulates in the open arena of the world. And this at once brings in important considerations.

The fœtus in the womb recapitulating the immense past (dreaming over again, if you like, the ancestral memories) can do so undisturbed (or comparatively so) by outer events, and can thus keep pretty closely along the line of its proper evolution. But the insect, commencing first as a primitive cell-like egg, then developing to a mere grub, then becoming a caterpillar or aquatic larva, with spiracles in the one case or gills in the other, then turning to a butterfly or winged image, has to pass through all these stages in the face of the outer world, and exposed to its severe competition and criticism ; and it is obvious that under these circumstances the line of its growth may be deflected, and may no longer quite coincide with the line of ancestral evolution.

Among the winged or partially winged insects, the *Orthoptera* (Grasshoppers, Cockroaches, Earwigs, &c.) and the *Hemiptera* (Bugs, Pond-skaters, Aphides, &c.) are considered, I believe, to be those whose line of growth has been least deflected in this way, and whose changes consequently best represent the sequence of ancestral evolution. These two orders are looked upon as very primitive, and probably nearer than any others to the wingless ancestors of the insect tribe.[1] Their wings, or such rudiments as they may possess, grow quite slowly, and are acquired in successive moults, without any distinct pupa stage. We may, therefore, suppose that there was a time when their ancestors had no wings, and not passing beyond the creeping and

[1] See F. M. Balfour's "Embryology." Lubbock agrees with Darwin in regarding *Campodea*, a certain insect of the wingless kind which passes through no metamorphoses, as representing the original stock whence all insects sprang.

crawling stage of existence, bred and propagated in that stage. Subsequently, however, some of the species developed membranous appendages which, with the aid of the wind, enabled them to skip and traverse the ground quickly; and, later still, these became perfect wings. The period of fertility was naturally delayed to the winged stage, on account of the advantages of widespread propagation, &c., and each individual insect now—recapitulating the life-history of the race—begins to acquire wings as it approaches maturity.

The *Orthoptera* and *Hemiptera*, however, being insects which do not use their wings to any great degree, have not been very much modified by such use, and consequently, as said, they have kept very much along the ancestral line of growth. But when we come to insects like Butterflies, Bees, Gnats, Dragon-flies, &c., which in their final stage almost live on the wing, it is obvious that, owing to this fact, their structure in the final stage has been greatly altered from the previous stages, and a kind of gap created between. The Butterfly must have a light body; it must have a suctorial proboscis instead of mandibular jaws; a complex eye adapted to long range, instead of the simple eye of the caterpillar, and so forth. Furthermore, the gap between it and the caterpillar may be widened by a thousand changes of condition and environment acting on the latter which were unknown to its predecessors. Among these may be reckoned the fact that the necessity of fertilisation being removed from the caterpillar stage to a later one, the caterpillar would no longer need to go actively about in search of a mate, thus exposing itself to dangers, but would rather adopt a policy of quiet ease and concealment. Thus it might easily grow to a much greater size than its ancestral type, and take on changes of form and habit which would lead it away from the old line of evolution. In this way, for example, the great gap and difference, in size and colour and every respect, between the caterpillar of the privet-hawk-moth and the perfect insect itself might be accounted for.

But the gap between the two stages having once appeared or begun to appear, an intermediate or pupal stage would be the necessary result. For, to take the last-mentioned instance, the caterpillar endeavouring to develop along the line of its racial memory, and yet having strayed somewhat from the ancestral tradition, would find, when the time came for its wings to appear, that it was off the track somehow, that its body had grown too big and lumbering for flight, that its skin was too thick perhaps for wing-formation, that its jaws, with continual exercise, had become too horny and monstrous to be possibly adapted for sipping honey, and so forth. What would it do? What could it do? It could not go on indefinitely in its new line as a gigantic caterpillar, for experience and memory would give it no clue how to do this. On the other hand, its whole racial instinct would be surging up within it in the direction of flight. What would it do? What could it do? Clearly, it could only give up its errant and strayed larval life as a bad job, coil up, and try to dream itself back again into its racial memory, and the proper line of its evolution. It could but refuse to eat, bring its existing career to a close, seek some retired spot, and withdrawing deep within itself, allow its wings to grow as quickly as may be, its overgrown jaws and digestive apparatus to shrivel and disappear, its old skin to harden and fall off, and the interrupted order of its evolution to be resumed. This then is what it does; and this is its pupal or chrysalis stage.

The pupal stage is an exaggeration of the ordinary moult, and is caused by a certain discontinuity which has arisen in the course of time between the larval and imaginal stages. It is a stage of internal changes, by which the continuity of development is recovered, and it resembles in some respects an effort of memory.

The necessity of quiescence during this stage is

involved (at least in most cases) by the nature of the changes taking place. It is evident, for instance, that the transformation of mouth-parts must mean a considerable period without food. Similarly, the casting of the old skin, and the formation of a new one, with fresh attachments for new muscles and organs, must mean temporary retirement and unfitness for the world. The pupal stage is like Memory; it is an abandonment of present complications, in order to knit on again to the long chain of the past. It is like Sleep; changes are going on in it, often rapidly enough, but they are of an internal character, and must not be interfered with by the outer world. It is like Death; for indeed large tracts of the old creature die, and other tracts take on a new life. And it is like Disease; for revolutions are in process within, the balance of centres is displaced and re-created, and for the time discomfort and uneasiness prevail.

The transformations of the animate world are, as I have said, endless. They are not confined to insects. It is sufficient to mention in this connection the extraordinary facts of asexual reproduction, alternate generation, and pelorism, to show how widely the principle ramifies. Of the higher vertebrates and Man, every individual goes through transformations, not only in the womb before birth, but afterwards in its proper and external life. In the case of Man, the transformations connected with teething, with puberty, and with the lapse of the sexual functions in age, are so considerable, and the disorganisation and readjustment of centres so great, that the change has often the appearance, and is accompanied by collateral symptoms, of Disease. And the query is suggested to us whether some illnesses which occur, and which leave patients greatly changed in temperament, and even improved in health, should not be looked on as natural and necessary accompaniments of some quite normal transformation which is going on deep below the surface, and as steps *forward* in the line of evolution, rather than as mere backslidings and signals of failure. As to Sleep, we may almost regard each night's rest as a brief pupal stage, for certain it is that every human being, man and woman, and especially boy and girl, comes again into the world each morning subtly transformed; something has passed into or out of their faces; a veil of thinnest texture has fallen from their souls. And when one thinks of it, one sees that Sleep is a state which allies itself easily to the condition of the chrysalis. For, however far we have travelled from our normal line of growth during the day, whatever wild excursions we have made into the regions of care and folly, the night's rest restores us, as we say, to our true selves, and we take up again the thread of our proper activity. In fact, in sleep we lapse more into the domain of racial memory; primitive instincts and thoughts come to the front in our dreams, and we are refreshed by bathing, as it were, in the morning dew of our own natures.

But this flooding of the soul with its own primitive life and instinct is most marked of all in the period of puberty. Strange that accompanying the physical changes which then take place in the body should occur this drenching of the mind in a sea of emotions and thoughts and fancies unknown to the child. It is as if a world of race-memories and experiences hitherto forgotten were suddenly recalled. The old infantile objects of pursuit and interest fade away; the whole perspective of the world is changed. Plato, of course, insists that Love is a reminiscence; the mania of Love is caused by the vision opening back in the soul once more of that celestial world, and of those divine forms and beings, which in ages past it had once beheld. We may or may not agree with Plato; but in any case it is interesting to find that he relates this powerful force, transforming the lives and fates of human beings to Memory, and looks upon the changes so induced as a renewal (may we say a recapitulation?) of a long-past existence.

Apart from puberty, apart from illnesses, apart from sleep, there are other periods, more obviously mental in their origin, of strange transformation in our lives—periods not unlike those of the "conversions" of religious folk—when after weeks or months of mental depression and lethargy, or of inward conflict and strain, or even of accompanying physical illness and incapacity, the whole nature seems to veer round and organise itself about new centres of interest and activity, and a sudden joy and outbreak of fresh life occurs. In these cases, taking the thing from the psychological side, we shall generally find that the impression produced on the mind is that it has found a long-lost key, that it has come *back* to something deep within itself. We speak of the return to Nature, return to Self, to Truth, to God, as if we were remembering something forgotten and neglected—taking up a broken thread; and the idea is suggested to us (though we cannot call it more than a suggestion) that the great well-springs of growth and transformation are indeed within; and that the successive stages of our human life are but the falling away of larval husks, which in time must disclose an universal Form. The allegory of the beautiful winged psyche—the very idealisation of life and love, delivered from the crawling worm and the cold, unpleasant chrysalis—has haunted the imagination of mankind from earliest times, kindling within it an immortal hope; and even the cold light of Science leaves it clear that in every creature sleeps this impetus of transformation towards an ever-wider range and capacity of life.

To come back to our particular May-fly. It is quite probable that this, and the other winged insects which emerge from the waters, were not originally aquatic, for in an aquatic life such insects could never have *learned* to acquire wings.[1] It was probably *after* the great body of Insects had acquired wings that the larvæ of some of these found themselves in marshy surroundings, and ultimately became adapted to an aquatic life. Then, though deeply changed and modified by their subaqueous existence, the memory and habit of wing-growth still came back upon them at its appointed time, and urged them once more to a terrestrial and aërial habitat. Thus the May-fly was able, and is able to-day, to effect that marvellous transfiguration from a watery grub to an aërial fairy which so astonishes us, as with an exhibition of strange determination and evolutionary force in so slight a creature. It is not only, as we have seen, the *extent* of the transfiguration, but the rapidity of it, which is surprising, and the cause of this final rapidity is the fact that the change has to be made in the presence and before the eyes, as it were, of the insect's most implacable foe and pursuer—the Trout! Whether as a larva in its bank-side burrow, or as the perfect image in the air, the Trout loves the May-fly; and if the latter delayed for a moment, even over the unbuttoning of its last garment, it would inevitably be snapped up. We may wonder that, under such circumstances, it did not give up the game long ago; but, in truth, though so innocent looking, the May-fly is an old hand, and this illusive little thing, that we call the creature of an hour, has really for thousands of centuries been practising her magic trick; and now so perfect is she in it that even

[1] Other reasons for believing that the aquatic Insects were originally terrestrial are (1) the common persistence of air-tubes and spiracles in aquatic insects; (2) that the most primitive forms of insects are terrestrial rather than aquatic; (3) that the aquatic species are more closely related to terrestrial species than to each other. (See Miall's "Nat. Hist. Aquatic Insects," pp. 4 and 5.)

while he, her enemy, is swimming towards her, darting from the dusky depths of his pool, she has already slipped her shroud, and is soaring in the eye of the sun.

After seeing that, one can but conclude that there is nothing that Man or other Creature may not do, provided he only chooses.

II

HEALTH A CONQUEST[1]

It is an important thought that health cannot be won without some amount of effort; that conquest and the putting forth of *power* are intimate conditions of its acquirement and preservation. Health—like freedom—has to be won afresh every morning.

And this in its way is true on all planes. In physical matters the effort of the muscles—exercise—is necessary to keep the body in good condition. In the mind, effort, or the mental faculties deteriorate. In morals again, effort—conscience, duty, sacrifice—all necessary.

This is a truth, or a side of the truth, which is worth dwelling on, especially in consideration of the fact that the easy tendency—the downhill grade—is all the other way: in the direction, namely, of a reliance on external props and supports—drugs, regulated stimulants, careful avoidance of draughts, plentiful flannels, and all the other paraphernalia of valetudinarianism.

"Now Roderick dear, remember, do,
Those breezes from the Channel,
And at the Volunteer Review
Please *don't* forget your flannel."

Not that the wise man despises flannels and the paraphernalia generally, but he remembers that they, poor things, can only give a kind of passive assistance—he

[1] Reprinted from *Seedtime*, April, 1892.

must do the real fighting himself—and salvation in the long run does not come by trusting to them.

Paradoxical as it may sound, Health demands for its continuance a certain willingness to run risks—even to forget itself—and so differs *toto coelo* from valetudinarianism, which is always occupied with its own safety. Strong exposure—to face the elements, the rain, the wind, the sun, extreme heat, extreme cold—to battle and overcome them, and take their strength into ours, like the Indian warrior who hangs the scalps of his slain to his girdle—that is good. Not to be done all at once, certainly; but to be done—in time. I would not say "Be foolish or rash"; but surely it is itself the height of rashness *not* to run a risk now and then, hiding ourselves as we do all day behind innumerable mufflers and the torn-off skins of animals, and in our stuffy dens, till we turn sickly pale all over like unwholesome crickets, and verily fear to venture out, lest she, Nature, the argus-eyed, see us and slay us in her wrath.

Why indeed do we dread a cold, a chill, so much, but because we are guilty within, and we know it—and the prowling influenza will find us out and expose our wickedness. It is good to be in such a state of health that you can sit or lie out, and turn cold, very cold—feel like a stone all over—and then thaw again and be none the worse. Not much of a miracle either, since even the poor beasts perform it, lying out in damp places or in frost every night! But their consciences no doubt burn clear and undimmed, affording a perpetual spring of inner warmth.

I knew a miner from Manitoba—and a good wholesome man he was—who told me that one night a stranger knocked at the door of his log-cabin on the edge of Lake Superior and begged help, saying that he and a companion had been crossing the lake on the ice, and that the companion had given out. He who knocked at the door had come on alone for assistance.

My friend picked up a lantern, and the two hurried down across the ice. The night was very cold and dark, but after some searching they found the man. He was lying stretched frozen and insensible and "stiff as a log." They picked him up and carried him back to the cabin, and sat up all night and into the next day continually rubbing and chafing his body. At last he came to and made a complete recovery, and in a few days—except for some marks of frost-bite on his skin—showed no sign of damage. Surely that was a holy man, in whom the frost, though it went right through his body, could find no sin.

It seems as if effort, or vigorous action, has the effect of *unifying* the body—making it whole under the stress of a single impulse—as if, through effort, the real being from within descended and made himself manifest. How often it happens, when one feels sick and out of sorts, that a call upon his energies rouses the man—he throws himself into the work, concentrates all his forces into one, and lo! when the rush of action is over he is quite well. It is a common remark that when people in old age give up their 'business' they soon die—the concentration of will ceasing, the body begins to break up. Sometimes when one sees people going about shivering on a cold day, enveloped in furs, weighed down with wrappings so that they can indeed only move slowly, one thinks how good it would be for most of them just to strip then and there, and *run*, run till they were red hot—mastering the cold that way. [Not an altogether gracious sight perhaps, as the mass of people are nowadays, with their pasty white skins and ineffectual movements—but all that would soon improve as they turned a more wholesome colour!] How strong it would make them feel, how secure! What new waves of Health never known before, rushing through the body! Then they might get clothed and return to their right minds again at leisure.

Appendix II

This evil (of putting all one's trust in external defences) is an evil which, like lying, reduplicates and complicates itself. The more clothes and wrappings you wear the slower and more feebly you move, also the more sensitive and 'nesh' does the skin become. Hence greater liability to chill, and necessity for *more* clothes, and so *ad infinitum.* Some of our good 'ladies,' under the enormous weight of sealskins, &c., which they feebly animate, seem to have reached the *infinitum* already.

The principle of conquest as to Health holds somehow also in regard to Food. There seem to be two views of food, more or less unconsciously entertained of course—and corresponding to them I think perhaps you may note two quite different manners or methods in eating.

The one view is that food is a mere material of health and strength—a material which has to be utilised, selected, controlled, and by some judicious power built up into the structure of the body ; the other, that food itself contains the forces which build up the body, and that *it* is the prime agent in the body's construction and renovation. The first gives the eater an active relation to his food, the second a passive ; the first tends towards, or somewhat in the direction of abstemiousness, the second in the direction of stimulants. I do not say that one is absolutely right and the other absolutely wrong, or that one is reasonable and the other quite unreasonable ; but I think that now that we have attained a state of civilisation in which speed in the chase is not for most of us an indispensable condition of getting our dinner, the first view is the one which we are most liable to overlook.

The digestive apparatus is like a sort of General Post Office—and a great deal of work to be done ; the food to be dissected and distributed—every atom of it sorted and sent to its different destination. What an innumerable activity is here! all the myriad different organic or chemic particles to be dealt with, each after its kind ; all the countless needs of the body to be provided for! Yet a healthy body has somehow, it would seem, the power of carrying on this complex process with extraordinary tact, authority and discrimination—determining quite decisively the amount and kind of food it requires, and sending every particle to its right place. This is indeed a conquest. The creature advances on the world, wrests from the general currents of the globe just those elements which it requires, and commands, nay compels them, to array themselves around it in obedience to some law or order, of which *we*—we I say who take such intimate part in the process—are still only dimly conscious. Nevertheless the order and the law *is* in our consciousness—or in regions which in time if not now will be accessible to our consciousness.

This apparatus of digestion, as we well know, can quite possibly be broken down by overloading it with work. And there is no doubt that all food beyond what is really needed is not only waste in itself but actually wastes energy in the disposal of it—destroys force instead of creating it. That the assimilation of food is work and involves the exertion of power is I think obvious to every one. (Hence, for instance, the need of warmth and quiet after meals.) Indeed there seems to be something necessary and radical in this idea: because the 'I,' the real person, can only, one would suppose, appear and become manifest through some *authentic* action, some action of its own; and if the body were constructed and built up by another force, not the ego—as, for instance, by the forces residing in the food—then would the body cease to be an expression or manifestation of such ego, and become rather a concealment and cloud over it.

That the bodies of many people, and of us all in degree, are built up in this external way; and are more or less clouded and spotty, I do not for a moment doubt. And here is the justification of the view that eating is a passive process. Shovel the curry and rice in, and let it sort itself! Let us have plenty of 'support'; give us active stimulating viands which will do the work themselves and save us the trouble of co-ordination, pick-me-ups which will restore animation at any hour, and always everything so well cooked that digestion may be rendered next to useless! In these moods we eat hastily, greedily, with little discrimination—as if in fear lest we should faint before the precious sustenance were well down our throats; and like all that is done in haste the work done at such times is not good work.

For what if by rendering digestion passive the power of making a true body has been lost? What if by trusting the nourishment to help *us*, instead of in ourselves to raise the nourishment to a higher plane of activity, we have put ourselves second and the lower forces first? Doubtless there are constructive forces resident in food, but what if these, instead of being dominated and controlled by the consuming organism, have been left to their own sweet will? Then a body truly has been built up, but not a human body—only the body of the sheep or the hog or of some other creature according to the nature of the food in question.

Here we have an interesting point. There is warfare, a struggle for supremacy, between me and that which I endeavour to assimilate. I am a man and I try to assimilate a sheep. What will the result be, man or sheep? Will my food assimilate *me*, by any chance? Yet this in plain terms is the warfare that is always going on, in every department of human life—the veritable struggle for existence; "the price of freedom (from sheephood) is eternal Vigilance."

In these lights the questions of animal and vegetable food, of cooked and raw, acquire a certain significance. Animal food, containing as it does highly wrought organic forces, may liberate within our system powers which we may find it difficult or even impossible to dominate—lethargic monsters, foul harpies, and sad-visaged lemures

—which may insist on having their own way, building up an animal body not truly human. The common-sense experience of all advanced races is against the use of *raw* animal food. We know its dangers too well. We do not want to make our bodies nests for *trichinae* or any other insubordinate forms. Cooked flesh is safer—a certain grade of vitality being destroyed by cookery—but then Oh, dear! if the lemures and harpies are dead, what kind of cheer is to be got out of their wretched carcases?

The passivity of the vegetable kingdom lends itself perhaps more readily to a true assimilation. But here on the other hand appears an opposite danger. The man who feeds on mere meek pulses and porridges may dominate them almost too easily. The reins of his chariot may grow slack and he himself quiescent, like a carter asleep behind an aged mare. Fresh fruits have more vitality in them; there are charming fragrant sylphs and oreads in these, which we seem to absorb into ourselves—and which it is a sin to drive out by fire. In a clean human body they love to dwell, making their homes there and finding plenty of occupation under the eye of the master. The slight indigestibility which some people complain of in raw fruit, nuts, and so forth, is a bit of a sign which these dainty little spirits make to us—a kind of challenge that we should effect that conquest of them which is their beatitude and our good Health.

In England and Germany of late years the movement towards sun-baths and open-air cures, and simplifications of dress generally, has taken great proportions. *Sandow's Magazine* not long ago (Jan. 1900) contained an article on the importance of open-air swimming-baths, with running track and gymnastic appliances combined. Such places (made as ornamental as may be, with shrubs and trees) would afford the immense advantage of work in the open, and of deep and free breathing—while the boon to the gymnast of being able to take a bath before dressing, or a run after swimming, would be obvious. "In truth there are few days in the year when such a place could not be used with advantage. Any runner knows that he can run through wintry weather or rain and feel 'as warm as a toast'—a good deal warmer than when shivering over the fire in a great-coat; and to conquer cold in this way, and get warm in spite of it, is splendid practice; and the mere fact of having done it once keeps one warm for the rest of the day. Like Thoreau, who said that one sack of coals served him all the winter—because when cold he simply carried the sack up from the cellar and took it down again; and this kept him warm without a fire!"

Certainly the exposure of the skin to sun and air is one of the most important conditions of health; and I believe that what we call 'catching cold' is greatly due to our everlastingly covering it, and so checking the action of its innumerable glands.

III

EVENING IN SPRING

A MEDITATION[1]

Most lovely is the evening. The swallows darting to and fro in a clear sky, the level shafts of the setting sun throwing into relief all the dimples and contours of the valley and its woods, the trail of blue smoke from a cottage floating slowly eastward, the massed blue-bells (like pools of water) in all the shady spots, under trees or along the wall sides, the faint fragrance, the outline of leaves overhead against the light, above all the wonderful sense of space, filled as it seems with the faintest mist—all so harmonious, calm, perfect. For a moment one envies the swallows their happiness, or the gnats dancing in the last sun-rays.

But the swallows are not happy. Little things they are rushing to and fro, consumed at every moment by the desire to catch a gnat—from one gnat to another they rush. If the swallow is happy it does not know that it is happy, it only knows that it has caught the gnat or that it has failed to catch it. One cannot call this happiness.

Or the gnat—whether it is caught or whether it escapes—one cannot call this happiness.

Or the blue-bell—whether among the thousands of other blue-bells down in that hollow it has succeeded in lifting its head to the coveted sun and air, or whether it

[1] Reprinted from *Seedtime*, April 1897.

has been choked, trampled out, by the huge crowd of its competitors, and lies there done to death beneath the dead leaves, a starveling bulb with an abortive shoot—one cannot call that happiness.

Or I—whether I have caught my gnat or whether I have failed to catch it; whether I have escaped my pursuer or whether I have failed to escape; whether I have trampled on others or whether I have myself been trampled on—I cannot call any of these things happiness.

And the scene is made up of swallows and gnats and blue-bells and human and other beings—thousands and thousands of them—therefore where among them all is happiness?

Yet happiness is there. When I look upon the scene I feel it is there; I know it. Indeed I feel it, unanswerable, incontestable, deep down, far below failure and success, in myself. It is something that cannot fail. It is in the life of the scene itself—of which life the little motives of the swallows and the gnats are the merest fractions.

Sometimes it seems horrible that Nature should be "a world of plunder and prey"—but then again it is not horrible. It is in no way horrible to me to think that one corpuscle in my circulation may swallow another; indeed it may be absolutely necessary for my body's existence that they should act so. If the corpuscle that is swallowed thinks he is ill-treated, and the corpuscle that swallows thinks that his merit has at last been rewarded, they are both under an illusion—the illusion that they exist in my circulation as separate individuals, and that my body is their happy hunting ground; and the sooner they get over that illusion the better:—

> "If the red slayer thinks he slays,
> And if the slain thinks he is slain,
> They know not well the subtle ways
> I keep, and pass, and turn again."

Evening in Spring: a Meditation

In this scene to-night there is a life which equalises individual fortune and misfortune. One blue-bell bulb must fail in order that another may succeed, but to that life there is neither failure nor success. The individual life has its pains and pleasures, which in the long run just about balance each other. The universal life is an eternal and surpassing joy, of which the other is but the nutriment and body.

The curious thing is, however, that one should be able to feel this universal life in one. The curious thing is that one should be prompted to say: "This, this surpassing existence is after all Myself, my true self." I wonder if the swallows and the gnats and the corpuscles of the blood have any inkling that they are really not mutually exclusive individuals; it seems as if there were two consciousnesses, more or less distinct and separable, in each person—one which occupies itself with the relation of things primarily to oneself as distinct from other persons; the other, more latent and less defined, which occupies itself with things as considered rather in relation to the common life of all. This latter consciousness has an abode of course in the individual, and perceives and acts through the individual, yet it cannot quite be called individual in its aims or judgments.

The curious thing is, I say, that this deeper, more universal consciousness should be a part of our actual selves. Yet that it is so there is no doubt. Hidden or clouded though it may be, yet it is recognisable to some degree in all men—nay, I believe that it is the very foundation of our individual life.

In the animals the universal life is strong (as witness their instincts often leading to sacrifice of their own existence), but it is unconscious, at least as far as *they* are concerned—or only quite subconscious. Their individual consciousness on the other hand, though keen and intense enough, is limited in area. In man the individual consciousness has grown so vast that it threatens—at a certain period of his development—to wrest him from universal ends in Titanic revolt against the Gods (a thing inconceivable in the case of the animals); but his salvation comes inevitably, in the growth also within him of a universal consciousness—the double consciousness bringing terrible discord and doubt for a time, till at last the fusion of the two, and the recognition of the primacy of the latter, restores harmony and makes his entrance into real life and happiness possible.

To attain this fusion of the individual and universal consciousness—so that, still remaining individual, one should partake and be aware of the universal life—this is the long effort and upward climb of humanity, worth all the struggles and disasters and failures by the way that may attend it. That in the process the thwarting, disappointment, and even partial destruction of the individual life should occasionally be necessary—in order that the germs of the higher consciousness may develop—seems a matter easy to understand. But when the process is complete the two sides of Man do but feed each other mutually—the universal nourishing and directing the individual, and the individual giving selfness and definition to the universal.

THE END

Printed by BALLANTYNE, HANSON & Co.
Edinburgh & London

Works by Edward Carpenter

GEORGE ALLEN
PUBLISHER · LONDON
RUSKIN HOUSE
156 · CHARING · CROSS · ROAD

Made in the USA
Las Vegas, NV
24 October 2021

32988757R00151